Stories from the Quran

Inspirational Tales of Faith and Guidance for Kids

Aasma S.

My First Picture Book Inc

Copyright © 2024 by My First Picture Book Inc.

All rights reserved.

No portion of this book may be reproduced in any form without written permission from the publisher or author, except as permitted by U.S. copyright law.

Contents

Introduction	1
1. Adam and Eve's Big Lesson	4
2. Noah and the Amazing Ark	8
3. Abraham and His Sons' Adventure	12
4. Moses and the Great Journey	16
5. Joseph's Colorful Dreamcoat	20
6. Solomon and the Queen of Sheba	26
7. David and the Goliath	30
8. Jonah and the Giant Fish	34
9. Job's Test of Faith	38
10. Mary and the Miracle of Baby Jesus	42
11. Ishmael and the Blessed Well	46

12.	Lot and the People of Sodom	50
13.	The Sleepers of the Cave	54
14.	The People of the Elephant	58
15.	The Two Sons of Adam	62
16.	Dhul-Qarnayn's Journey to Help	66
17.	The Story of Bravery and Belief	70
18.	Moses and Khidr's Adventures	74
19.	The Garden of Sharing	78
20.	The Rich Man's Lesson	82
21.	Solomon and the Tiny Teachers	86
22.	Prophet Hud and the Windy City	90
23.	The Marvelous Camel of Salih	94
24.	The Garden of Greed	98
25.	Shuaib and the Town of Madyan	102
26.	King Solomon's Missing Advisor	106
27.	Moses and the Wise Fisherman	110

28.	Abraham and the Broken Idols	114
29.	The Miracles of Prophet Elisha	118
30.	Prophet Muhammad's Adventure	122
31.	Moses and the Talking Stone	126
32.	Prophet Elias and the Fire	130
33.	The Day the Sun Stood Still	134
34.	Prophet Zakariya and John	138
35.	Moses and Aaron's River Rescue	142
36.	Prophet Idris and the Angel Gabriel	146
37.	Isaiah and the Special Message	150
38.	King Solomon's Flying Carpet	154
39.	Muhammad and the Spider	158
40.	King Solomon and the Playful Jinn	162
41.	Moses and the Twelve Springs	166
42.	The Wise Words of Muhammad	170
43.	The Journey to Mecca	174

44.	Moses and the Golden Calf	178
45.	Moses and the Sweet Spring	184
46.	Muhammad and the Unity Pact	188
47.	Abraham's Journey of Faith	192
48.	Moses and the Missing Robe	196
49.	Luqman's Lessons of Wisdom	200
50.	Moses and the Scared Servant	204

Introduction

Welcome to **Stories from the Quran: Inspirational Tales of Faith and Guidance for Kids**! This book is a collection of wonderful stories adapted from the Quran, written especially for young readers. Each tale is filled with wisdom, kindness, and important lessons that help us understand the values of faith and good conduct.

In these pages, you will find stories about brave prophets, wise leaders, and miraculous events. Each story has been lovingly rewritten in simpler English and with gentle language to make them perfect for children. We've taken care to ensure that the messages of these timeless tales are clear and inspiring, without any harsh or difficult parts that might be too much for young minds.

As you read these stories, you will journey through deserts, valleys, and mountains, meet fascinating characters, and witness amazing miracles. Most importantly, you will learn about the values of patience, kindness, honesty, and the importance of having faith in Allah.

We hope these stories will inspire you and fill your heart with joy and wonder. May they bring you closer to understanding the beauty and wisdom of the Quran.

Happy reading!

Chapter 1

Adam and Eve's Big Lesson

Once upon a time, in a magical garden filled with bright flowers and tasty fruits, there was a special place made by God. This garden was called Paradise, and it was a happy place, always filled with laughter and joy.

God decided to make the first two people to enjoy this wonderful garden. He first made Adam from the soil of the Earth. Adam was kind and clever. Seeing that Adam needed a friend to share the fun of the garden, God then made Eve from Adam, making them the best of friends.

In this amazing garden, God had one big rule. He told Adam and Eve they could eat the fruit from any tree in the garden, except for the fruit from one special tree right in the middle of the garden. God explained that this tree was different, and they should not eat its fruit or even touch it.

Adam and Eve had a lot of fun in the garden! They played with the animals, swam in the rivers, and ate tasty fruits from all the trees, except for the one tree God had told them to stay away from.

But one day, while they were near that special tree, a sneaky snake talked to Eve. The snake tricked her by saying if they ate the fruit from this tree, they would be as wise as God. Eve believed the snake and picked the fruit. She ate it and also gave some to Adam, who ate it too.

Right after they ate the fruit, they realized they had made a big mistake. They felt sad and scared because they had not listened to God's rule. When God found out, He was very unhappy because Adam and Eve had not followed His one rule. Because of this, God decided they couldn't stay in the beautiful garden anymore.

Adam and Eve were very sorry for what they had done. They said sorry to God for not listening to Him. Even though they had to leave Paradise, God still loved them a lot. He gave them clothes to wear and promised to take care of them wherever they went.

So, Adam and Eve left the garden and started a new life outside. It wasn't easy at first; they had to learn how to do everything themselves—like growing their own food and building their own home. But they worked together and learned many new things.

Outside the garden, Adam and Eve found a new world that was different from Paradise. They had to plant seeds to grow their food. They learned to take care of the plants and animals. They also built a cozy home to live in. Even though life was harder, they were happy to be together and to have God's love.

Adam and Eve had many children and taught them about God and the beautiful garden they once lived in. They told stories about their adventures in Paradise and reminded their children to always listen to God's guidance.

Moral of the Story:

Making good choices and listening to advice is very important. Adam and Eve learned that not following rules can lead to tough times, but they also learned that saying sorry and trying to do better can help us move forward with kindness and love from others.

Chapter 2

Noah and the Amazing Ark

Once upon a time, long ago, there was a kind man named Noah. He lived in a place where people forgot how to be nice to each other and take care of the Earth. Noah felt sad about this. He always tried to show them how to be better, but no one listened.

One day, God spoke to Noah. God told him that a big flood was coming because the people were not acting right. But God wanted to keep Noah, his family, and the good animals safe. So, God gave Noah a very special job: to build a huge boat called an ark.

Noah started working on the ark. It was huge and made of strong wood. He worked very hard, hammering and sawing wood every day. Even though people laughed at him and didn't believe a flood would come, Noah kept building because he believed God.

After many days, the ark was all set. It was like a big, giant house that could float on water! Then, God told Noah to bring all sorts of animals onto the ark. Just think about it! Lions, elephants, giraffes, bunnies, and even tiny ants came in pairs to the ark. Noah welcomed each and every one into the big boat.

He also brought his family inside the ark. They packed a lot of food and water because they didn't know how long they would need to stay inside. Just as they finished, the sky turned dark, and it began to rain. Soon, it was raining harder than anyone had ever seen before!

The rain kept pouring down, and the water got higher and higher until even the tallest mountains were under water. But Noah's ark was safe. It floated on the water, carrying Noah, his family, and all the animals.

Inside the ark, they stayed for many days and nights. It rained outside, and the wind blew, but inside, Noah made sure everyone was safe and had enough to eat. It was a bit scary and very noisy, but Noah's family and the animals knew they were safe in their big boat.

After a long time, the rain stopped, and the sun came out again. The water slowly started to go away. One day, Noah sent out a dove to see if there was dry land. The dove flew away but came back because it found nowhere to land. Noah waited a bit longer and sent the dove out again. This time, it brought back an olive leaf! That meant trees were growing again, and there was dry land.

Finally, when the earth was dry enough, God told Noah to open the ark. Everyone inside was so happy to get out! They stretched their legs and looked around at their new home. The animals went back to their homes in the forests and fields.

God was very pleased with Noah for being brave and faithful. To promise that He would never send such a big flood again, God put a beautiful rainbow in the sky.

Noah and his family started their new life on this clean earth. They planted seeds and grew gardens. They always remembered to be kind and take care of each other and the world around them.

Every time they saw a rainbow in the sky, they remembered God's promise and felt grateful for the new life they had been given. They knew that no matter what challenges they faced, they could overcome them by working together and staying true to their faith.

Moral of the Story:

Noah's story shows us it's important to be brave and trust even when others doubt us. It tells us to always care for our planet and each other. Every time we see a rainbow, let's think of Noah's big boat and God's promise of love and protection, reminding us that kindness and faith help us through the hardest times.

Chapter 3

Abraham and His Sons' Adventure

Once upon a time, under a sky full of twinkling stars, there lived a kind and wise man named Abraham. He loved looking at the stars and thinking about the big world. Abraham was known for his kind heart and strong faith in God.

God cared very much for Abraham because he believed so deeply. One day, God made a promise to Abraham that he would have as many children as the stars in the sky. This promise made Abraham very happy, but he was also surprised because he and his wife Sarah were quite old.

After some time, three special visitors came to see Abraham. These were not just any visitors; they were angels sent by God! They brought exciting news that Abraham and Sarah would soon have a baby boy. Sarah laughed when she heard this because she thought she was too old to have a baby. But the angels told her that with God, anything is possible.

Soon, the promise came true, and Sarah had a baby boy. They named him Isaac, which means "laughter," because Sarah laughed when she heard she would have a baby. Isaac grew up to be kind and wise, just like his dad.

Abraham also had another son named Ishmael, who was born before Isaac. Ishmael was brave and strong, and Abraham loved him very much. Both boys grew up learning about the stars, the desert, and trusting in God.

One day, God wanted to test Abraham's faith. He asked Abraham to take Isaac to a mountain far away. Abraham felt sad but trusted God. So, they traveled together—Abraham, Isaac, and their loyal donkey carrying wood.

When they got to the mountain, Isaac noticed they didn't have a lamb for a sacrifice. He asked his dad about it, and Abraham said that God would provide one. As Abraham prepared to show his faith, an angel stopped him! This was a test, and Abraham had shown his deep trust in God.

Right then, they saw a ram caught by its horns in a bush. God had provided a sacrifice, just as Abraham believed He would. Both father and son were thankful. They learned that having faith means trusting even when you're not sure what will happen.

God was very pleased with Abraham's faith. He blessed Abraham and reminded him that his children would be as numerous as the stars in the sky.

Abraham's sons, Isaac and Ishmael, grew up to be leaders who taught others about their father's faith. They spread love and kindness wherever they went, just like Abraham had taught them.

Moral of the Story:

Abraham's story teaches us that having faith is powerful. It shows us that we can face any challenge if we believe in promises and trust in our family's support. Whenever we see the stars at night, we can remember Abraham's faith and feel strong knowing we are never alone.

Chapter 4

Moses and the Great Journey

Once upon a time, in a land with big pyramids and huge deserts, there lived a kind man named Moses. Moses was chosen by God to do important things, but his story starts in a surprising way.

When Moses was a tiny baby, the Pharaoh of Egypt, who was very powerful and sometimes mean, made a rule that all new baby boys should not be allowed to grow up. This made Moses' mom very scared but also very brave. She believed in God's plan for her baby and put him in a basket on the river, hoping he would be safe.

The basket floated down the river until it was found by the Pharaoh's daughter. She saw the baby and loved him right away. She chose to raise him as her own, and that's how Moses grew up in the Pharaoh's big palace. He learned many things but never forgot where he came from.

As Moses got older, he saw that the people from his first home were being treated very badly and had to work really hard. Moses felt very sad and asked God to help him find a way to help these people.

One day, while Moses was looking after sheep in the desert, something amazing happened. He saw a bush that was on fire but wasn't getting burned up! From this incredible burning bush, God spoke to Moses. God told him to go back to Egypt and ask the Pharaoh to let his people go free. This was a big job, and Moses felt nervous, but he knew he had to try.

Moses went back to Egypt with courage. His brother Aaron, who was good at talking, helped him speak to the Pharaoh. Together, they told the Pharaoh exactly what God said: "Let my people go!" But the Pharaoh was very stubborn and said no. Because of this, Egypt had ten awful problems happen one after another. Rivers turned to blood, frogs were everywhere, and sometimes it was completely dark!

Each time something bad happened, Moses and Aaron asked the Pharaoh again, "Please let my people go." And every time, the Pharaoh would say no—until the last problem. It was so sad and scary that the Pharaoh finally said yes.

Moses led his people away from Egypt toward freedom. They walked for many days. When they got to a big sea called the Red Sea, they thought they were stuck. But Moses trusted God. He lifted his staff, and God did something incredible — He made the sea open up! The people walked across on dry ground with walls of water on both sides.

When they were all safely on the other side, the water went back to normal just as the Pharaoh's soldiers tried to follow. Moses and his people were safe, and they sang happy songs to thank God for the great miracle.

Moses kept leading his people through the desert to a land that God had promised them. Along the way, he taught them about God's rules and how to be kind to each other. They learned a lot from Moses about being brave, having faith, and keeping hope.

Finally, after many years of traveling, they reached the edge of the land that God had promised them. Moses was very old by then, but he was happy to see the beautiful land where his people would live. He knew that they were ready to build new lives there, following God's rules and living in peace.

Moral of the Story:

Being brave means doing the right thing even when it's very hard. Remember Moses' big journey whenever you face something tough—it's a story about courage, amazing miracles, and standing up for what is right.

Chapter 5

Joseph's Colorful Dreamcoat

Once upon a time, in a land surrounded by vast deserts and rich fields, there lived a boy named Joseph. Joseph was very special to his father Jacob, who loved him dearly. To show his love, Jacob gave Joseph a beautiful coat with many colors. It was so bright and cheerful that it made everyone smile.

Joseph had eleven brothers, but they were not happy about the colorful coat or the attention Joseph got from their father. Joseph also had dreams that he loved to share with his family. In one dream, he saw the sun, the moon, and eleven stars all bowing down to him. This dream made his brothers even more upset because they thought it meant Joseph would become very important, and they felt jealous.

One day, Joseph's brothers were taking care of sheep in a field far away. Their father, Jacob, asked Joseph to go check on them and see if they were alright. Eager to help, Joseph set off to find his brothers. But when his brothers saw him coming, their jealousy took over. They made a mean plan and threw Joseph into a deep, dark pit.

After some time, they felt a little sorry and didn't want to hurt him anymore. So instead, they lifted Joseph out of the pit and sold him to some traders traveling to Egypt. They told their father that a wild animal had hurt Joseph, showing him the colorful coat covered in goat's blood. Jacob was heartbroken, thinking he had lost his dear son.

In Egypt, the traders sold Joseph to a man named Potiphar. Even though he was far from home and his family, Joseph worked hard and was kind to everyone. God was with him, so everything he did went well. Potiphar noticed this and soon made Joseph in charge of his whole house.

But life had more challenges for Joseph. He was wrongly accused of doing something bad and was put in jail. Even in jail, Joseph was kind and wise, helping others and solving their problems. He even interpreted dreams for some of his fellow prisoners, just like he had done with his own dreams back home.

One day, the Pharaoh of Egypt had a dream that no one could understand. Hearing of Joseph's gift, the Pharaoh called him to the palace. Joseph listened to the Pharaoh's dream about skinny cows eating fat cows and explained that it meant Egypt would have seven years of lots of food followed by seven years of very little food. Joseph advised the Pharaoh to save food from the good years to use during the bad years.

The Pharaoh was so impressed by Joseph's wisdom that he made him a leader in Egypt, second only to himself. Joseph worked hard, collecting food in the good years and distributing it when the times were tough.

Years later, a great famine hit all the lands around Egypt, including where Joseph's family lived. His brothers came to Egypt looking for food, not knowing that the leader they would ask help from was Joseph! When he saw them, Joseph recognized his brothers immediately, but they did not recognize him.

Joseph tested his brothers to see if they had changed. After several tests, he could no longer hold back his feelings and revealed himself to his brothers. They were scared because of what they had done to him before, but Joseph forgave them. He understood that all his hardships were part of a bigger plan to save many people.

Joseph invited his whole family to live in Egypt where he could take care of them. When Jacob saw Joseph again, he was filled with joy. The family was reunited, and they all lived together happily in Egypt.

Moral of the Story:

Joseph's story teaches us that even when bad things happen, good can come out of it if we stay kind and forgive others. Like Joseph's colorful coat brought smiles, his story brings hope that everything can turn out well in the end.

Chapter 6

Solomon and the Queen of Sheba

Long ago, in a land with big gardens and busy markets, there lived a wise king named Solomon. King Solomon was a special king; he could understand what animals said and could even control the wind. Everyone knew him as a very wise and fair king.

One sunny day, while talking with birds, Solomon noticed that one bird, the hoopoe bird, was missing. When the hoopoe bird came back, it had exciting news from a faraway land where a kind and wise queen lived. This land was filled with gold and pretty stones, and the people there worshipped the sun instead of God.

Solomon wanted to help them learn about God, so he decided to send a letter to the Queen of Sheba. He gave the letter to the hoopoe bird to take to her. In the letter, he invited the queen to come and visit his kingdom to see how wise he was and to learn about God.

The queen was very interested when she got the letter. She thought a lot about it and decided to visit Solomon. She was very smart, so she planned to ask Solomon some tough riddles to see how wise he really was. She brought some very special gifts with her too.

After a long trip over mountains and deserts, the Queen of Sheba arrived at Solomon's beautiful palace. She was amazed by how grand it was. Solomon welcomed her and her people warmly.

During her visit, the queen asked Solomon many hard questions and riddles. Solomon answered all of them easily. His answers were smart and showed he understood a lot. The queen was very impressed, not just by his wisdom but also by how kind and fair he was to everyone and even to the animals.

Then, it was time for her special gifts. One of these gifts was a bouquet that looked just like real flowers but was actually made of glass. Solomon knew right away that they were not real flowers, which showed how observant he was.

The queen was so amazed by everything she saw and learned. She realized that Solomon's wisdom came from his strong faith in God. She started to believe in Solomon's God too and promised to share this knowledge with her own people.

Before she left, Solomon gave her many gifts to take back with her. They promised to stay friends and keep learning from each other. The winds helped her travel safely back home with her gifts and new knowledge.

Moral of the Story:

Being wise means more than just knowing a lot. It also means understanding others and helping them see what truly matters. Solomon's story shows us that real wisdom includes being smart, kind, fair, and good at sharing what we know to bring people together.

Chapter 7

David and the Goliath

Once upon a time, in a land with big deserts and ancient cities, there lived a young shepherd boy named David. David was small, but he was very brave and had a lot of faith in God. He spent his days outside under the sun, watching over his sheep and practicing throwing stones with his sling, which he used very well.

During this time, David's people, the Israelites, were having big troubles. They were fighting against a group called the Philistines, who were very tough. The Philistines had a giant warrior named Goliath. Goliath was so huge and strong that everyone was too scared to fight him. Each day, he would stand on a hill and yell at the Israelites, daring anyone to challenge him.

One day, David's father asked him to take some food to his brothers who were soldiers in the Israelite army. When David got to the camp, he saw Goliath yelling just like every other day. Goliath was making fun of the Israelites and their faith, and this made David feel that he needed to do something.

David felt it was his duty to stand up for his people and protect their honor. He said, "Why is this giant allowed to make fun of God's army?" Even though David was just a young boy, he believed that with God's help, he could defeat Goliath.

When the king of Israel heard about David's wish to fight the giant, he was surprised because David was so young and small. But David explained to the king how he had kept his sheep safe from lions and bears using only his sling and his faith. The king was impressed by David's bravery and agreed to let him fight, offering him armor and a sword to wear. But when David tried on the armor, he found it too heavy and awkward. So, he decided not to wear any armor and just took his sling and picked five smooth stones from a stream.

As David walked towards Goliath with his sling and stones, Goliath laughed out loud, thinking it was funny that a young boy was coming to fight him. But David wasn't scared at all. He trusted God to protect and guide him.

David put a rock in his sling, pulled back and then let go of one stone with all his might. Guided by his faith, the stone flew straight and hit Goliath right in the forehead. The giant fell down with a big thud. When the Philistines saw that their strongest warrior was defeated by young David, they were shocked and scared, and they ran away.

The Israelites cheered for David, who became their new hero. They learned that being big and strong isn't as important as being brave and having faith in God. David grew up to be a great leader, always remembering the day he defeated the giant with just his sling and a stone.

Moral of the Story:

David's story helps us learn that no matter how big our problems are, we can solve them if we are brave and trust in God. David shows us that even if we are small, we can do great things with faith and courage.

Chapter 8

Jonah and the Giant Fish

Once upon a time, in a land with shiny seas and golden sands, there was a man named Jonah. Jonah was kind and always tried to follow God, but one day, he made a big mistake. God asked Jonah to go to a city called Nineveh to help the people learn to be good, but Jonah was scared and ran away the other way.

Jonah jumped on a ship that sailed far across the deep blue sea. He thought he could escape from God by going far away. However, God was watching over him. While Jonah was on the ship, a huge storm started. The sea was wild, with big waves and strong winds. The sailors on the ship were very scared and prayed for safety, while Jonah knew he was running from his job. He understood the storm was happening because of him.

To keep everyone safe on the ship, Jonah told the sailors to throw him into the sea. They didn't want to, but they finally did what Jonah said, and as soon as Jonah splashed into the water, the storm stopped. The sea became calm, and the sailors were amazed.

But then, something amazing happened. God sent a giant fish to swallow Jonah whole. Inside the fish's belly, it was dark and smelly. Jonah was scared at first, but he prayed to God. He said he was sorry and promised to do his job if God helped him out. Jonah stayed inside the fish for three whole days and nights, thinking about his choices.

After three days, God made the fish spit Jonah out onto dry sand. Jonah was all wet but thankful to be safe. He knew he had to listen to God this time and go to Nineveh like he was supposed to.

Jonah walked to Nineveh and told everyone God's message. He explained that they needed to stop being mean and say sorry for their mistakes. To Jonah's surprise, the people of Nineveh listened to him! They really said sorry and started to change their ways.

When God saw that the people of Nineveh were trying to be better, He was happy. God decided to be kind and forgave them. He did not let anything bad happen to them. From this, Jonah learned how loving and forgiving God could be.

Jonah went back home, feeling thankful for God's kindness and happy he had done his task. He now understood that avoiding problems doesn't help; it only makes things harder. But if you face them and try to make things right, you can find peace and happiness.

Moral of the Story:

Jonah's story shows us why it's important to listen and do what's right, even when it's hard. It teaches us that saying sorry and fixing our mistakes can make things better. Always remember, it's never too late to change and do the right thing, and God is always ready to forgive us.

Chapter 9

Job's Test of Faith

Long ago, in a beautiful land filled with green fields and tall mountains, there lived a kind man named Job. Job loved God with all his heart and was thankful for his many blessings. He had a big, happy family, lots of animals, and a huge piece of land. Everyone knew Job as one of the kindest and richest men around.

One day, Satan came to God and started wondering about Job's love. He thought that Job loved God only because he had a good life. God knew that Job's love was true, and to show this, He allowed Satan to test Job but made sure that Job wouldn't be hurt too badly.

The test started when Satan took away all of Job's animals and crops. Suddenly, Job had very little left. Then, something even sadder happened—Job's children were taken away by terrible disasters. This broke Job's heart, but he did not stop loving God.

Next, Satan made Job very sick to see if that would make him stop loving God. Job felt awful, but he didn't give up. He kept praying and trusting God, even though he was in a lot of pain.

During this hard time, Job's wife and friends were worried. They didn't understand why Job kept his faith. They told him he might as well stop believing since he was suffering so much. But Job knew that God had a plan, and he chose to keep his faith strong.

Job was very patient. He wondered why all these bad things were happening to him, but he never got angry with God. He kept believing that God was good and that there must be a reason for everything.

Every day, Job prayed and thanked God for the things he still had. He would sit outside and look at the stars, remembering how big and wonderful God's creation was. Even though he was sad and in pain, he found comfort in knowing that God was with him.

After a long time of hardship, God spoke to Job. He explained that many things in the world are too complex for us to understand, but He is always with us, guiding and helping. God's words made Job feel better because he knew that God cared about him.

God was pleased with Job's faith. To show His happiness, God healed Job and gave him even more than he had before. Job's animals returned, and his land was full of crops again. God also gave Job a new family with many children. This new family was a gift of happiness, showing that after tough times, good things can come.

Job's life was full of joy once again. He lived for many more years, surrounded by his family and friends. He was grateful for every day and continued to share his love and blessings with everyone around him.

Moral of the Story:

Job's story teaches us that even when bad things happen, if we stay strong and believe, good things can come our way. We learn that being brave and trusting can help us through tough times, and we are never alone. Always remember, no matter how hard things get, there's always hope for happy days again.

Chapter 10

Mary and the Miracle of Baby Jesus

Long ago, in a land with beautiful gardens and old cities, there lived a kind young woman named Mary. Mary loved God very much and spent a lot of her time praying and finding peace in her heart. She was gentle and caring, always helping those in need.

One quiet day, while Mary was praying alone, something amazing happened. An angel from God came to see her. The angel had a very special message for Mary. He told her, "You will have a baby boy, and you will name him Jesus. He will bring God's love and kindness to the whole world."

Mary was surprised and felt very honored by this message. She knew this was a big responsibility but trusted in God's plan. Even though she was young and not yet married, Mary said yes to God's plan with all her heart.

As months went by, Mary's belly grew because baby Jesus was growing inside her. She and Joseph, who loved her dearly, prepared for the arrival of the baby. Joseph was a carpenter, and he made a small cradle for Jesus. They both knew that their baby was special and that he would need their love and care.

When it was almost time for Jesus to be born, Mary and Joseph had to travel to a town called Bethlehem. The journey was long and tiring, and Mary rode on a donkey while Joseph walked beside her. When they arrived in Bethlehem, they looked for a place to stay, but the town was very crowded. There was no room anywhere else, so they ended up in a small, cozy stable surrounded by animals.

That night, under a sky full of shining stars, Mary gave birth to Jesus. The stable felt warm and filled with light as the little baby arrived, bringing peace and joy. Mary held her new son close, amazed by the miracle of his birth. She wrapped him in soft cloths and laid him in the manger, a trough where animals eat.

Outside the stable, something wonderful was happening too. Shepherds in the fields nearby saw a bright, shining star in the sky. Suddenly, angels appeared, singing beautifully and telling them about the birth of a special baby who would bring joy to all. Excited and curious, the shepherds hurried to the stable to see baby Jesus. They brought simple gifts and knelt down to admire the baby, feeling blessed to be part of this miracle.

At the same time, far away in the East, some wise men noticed the same bright star. They knew it meant a great king had been born. These wise men traveled a long way, over mountains and through deserts, following the star to find Jesus. They brought with them gifts of gold, sweet frankincense, and myrrh, which were very precious. These gifts were symbols of their respect and love for the new baby.

When the wise men arrived at the stable, they saw baby Jesus and felt a great peace. They gave him their gifts and knew he was a very special baby. They bowed before him, knowing he was sent by God to bring love and kindness to the world.

Mary watched all this with joy and gratitude. She knew her baby was here to bring hope and happiness to the world. As Jesus grew up, he became wise and kind. He taught everyone about loving each other and being kind, just like he was. He made friends with everyone and helped those who were sad or in trouble. Jesus grew to be a man who spread love and kindness wherever he went.

Moral of the Story:

The story of Mary and baby Jesus teaches us about the wonderful things that can happen when we believe and trust in God. It shows us that love and kindness are very powerful and can change the world.

Chapter 11

Ishmael and the Blessed Well

ISHMAEL AND THE BLESSED WELL

Once upon a time, in a land filled with golden sands and vast deserts, there was a young boy named Ishmael. He was the cherished son of Abraham and Hagar. They lived in a desert near a special city called Mecca, where the great Kaaba, a sacred house, stood.

One day, God told Abraham to take Hagar and Ishmael to a lonely part of the desert. Abraham trusted God's plan, so he did as God told him, even though it was hard. He believed that God would take care of his family. So, Abraham left Hagar and Ishmael in the desert with just a little water and some food.

Soon, their water was all gone. The sun was very hot, and the sand was warm under their feet. Hagar looked at Ishmael, who was very thirsty, and she decided to look for water. She ran up and down between two hills called Safa and Marwah. She ran back and forth seven times, hoping to find some water or someone to help them.

After her last run, something amazing happened. An angel appeared! The angel touched the ground near where Ishmael was sitting. Suddenly, water started to bubble up from the sand. It was a miracle! This water was called Zamzam water. It was a special gift from God.

The water was cool and refreshing, and it saved Ishmael and his mother from being too thirsty.

The Zamzam Well, where the water came from, became a very important place. People from all around came to drink its water. It wasn't just any water; it was known to be very special and good for everyone who drank it.

As Ishmael grew up near the Zamzam Well, his mother taught him many important things. She told him about God's kindness and how important it is to trust God. Ishmael learned to be patient and grateful for everything he had. He also learned the story of how the angel had brought them the life-saving water.

Ishmael became very kind and wise as he grew older. He was friendly and generous to everyone he met. If travelers were passing by, tired and thirsty from walking in the desert, Ishmael would welcome them. He shared the Zamzam water with them and told them the story of how the well came to be.

Moral of the Story:

Ishmael's journey teaches us that having faith and helping others are very important. The story of the Zamzam Well reminds us that when we believe and help others, good things will happen. We can all be like Ishmael, sharing and caring for those around us.

Chapter 12

Lot and the People of Sodom

Once upon a time, in a beautiful land with rolling hills and wide valleys, a kind man named Lot lived. Lot loved God and always tried to be good and helpful. He lived in a city called Sodom, where people often forgot to be nice to each other and did not follow good manners.

Lot was sad because many around him were not kind. He wanted to help them be better, so he prayed a lot and never lost hope that his neighbors could change. Every day, Lot tried to show them how to be kind by being generous and caring himself. He would help anyone in need, give food to the hungry, and offer a kind word to those who were sad.

One sunny day, three special visitors came to Sodom. These visitors were angels sent from God, but they looked just like ordinary people. Lot saw them and invited them to his home. He was very hospitable, giving them food and a place to rest. He made them a delicious meal and treated them with great respect.

That night, the angels shared their secret mission with Lot. They had come to warn him because God was going to send a big punishment to the city for all the bad things people were doing. Lot was worried for his family and the people of Sodom.

As the sky turned dark, the people of Sodom, curious and unruly, gathered around Lot's house. They had heard about the strangers and demanded that Lot bring them out. Lot was worried but he bravely stood at his door. He tried to talk to the crowd, asking them to go away and not to hurt anyone. He wanted to protect his guests and help his neighbors understand that being mean was not right.

However, the people of the city wouldn't listen. They kept shouting and demanding to see the visitors. At that moment, the angels acted to protect Lot and his family. They made the crowd go blind, stopping them from causing any harm. The crowd stumbled around, confused and unable to find Lot's door.

Then, the angels told Lot to quickly gather his family and leave the city. They warned him not to look back because something very scary was about to happen. Lot, his wife, and their daughters left their home in the middle of the night. They hurried away from Sodom, guided by one of the angels.

As they were leaving, the sky behind them grew brighter and brighter. A loud noise boomed as fire began to fall from the sky. The entire city of Sodom was being destroyed because of the bad choices of its people. The ground shook, and the flames roared as they consumed the city.

Lot and his family reached a safe place, a cave in the hills. From there, they watched in shock as their city was consumed by flames.

Throughout everything, Lot's belief in being good and just never wavered. He knew that following what was right, even when it was hard, was very important. This helped him stay brave and keep his family safe. Lot and his family found a new place to live and started a new life.

Moral of the Story:

Lot's story teaches us that it is very important to stay true to what is right and to be kind, even when others are not. It shows us that good actions and faith can guide us safely through the toughest times.

Chapter 13

The Sleepers of the Cave

Once upon a time, in a land of tall hills and whispering forests, a group of young men known for their strong faith in God lived in a small village. These young men were called the Sleepers of the Cave because of the incredible miracle that happened in their lives.

The Sleepers of the Cave lived during a time when many people around them were choosing not to follow the good and kind ways taught by God. Instead, these people were making bad choices and forgetting to be nice to each other. The young men found it very hard to see this happening, but they never stopped believing in being good and kind.

Because the village was becoming a difficult place for them to live their good lives, they decided to find a quiet place where they could pray and talk to God without being disturbed. They found a big, old cave in the forest, which was perfect for their prayers. The cave was cool and quiet, a perfect place to find peace and speak to God.

One day, a very mean king started ruling the land. This king didn't believe in God and wanted everyone to only praise him and follow his mean ways. He ordered everyone to stop being kind and to forget about God. But the Sleepers of the Cave refused to follow the king's orders because they wanted to stay true to their faith in God.

Knowing that they were not safe, the young men went into their cave to hide. They prayed to God to protect them from the king. God heard their prayers and decided to keep them safe in a very special way. He put them into a deep sleep inside the cave.

While they slept, something amazing happened. Even though days and years passed, the sun moved across the sky but its rays never touched the Sleepers directly, so they remained comfortable and safe in their gentle sleep. This was a miracle that kept them just right—not too warm and not too cold.

Years turned into many decades, and the mean king was long gone, replaced by a kind ruler who believed in being good and kind like the Sleepers. One day, the new king and his people discovered the old cave. They were curious about the stories they had heard and wanted to see if the Sleepers were real.

When the cave was finally opened, the Sleepers of the Cave woke up. They hadn't aged a day, and they were surprised to find that so many years had passed. The people who saw them wake up were amazed and realized that this was a sign of God's power and His care for those who believe in Him.

The story of the Sleepers of the Cave spread quickly and became a symbol of hope and faith. It showed everyone that no matter how tough things get, staying true to good values and believing in God can lead to miraculous protection.

Moral of the Story:

The Sleepers of the Cave teach us the power of faith and staying true to what is right. Their story helps us remember that even when things are tough, we can always rely on God's protection and love. Just like the Sleepers, our faith can give us strength and keep us safe.

Chapter 14

The People of the Elephant

Once upon a time, in a land filled with tall palm trees and stretches of golden sands, there was a very powerful king who wanted to tear down a special building called the Kaaba in the city of Mecca. This king had a mighty army, and in that army, there was an enormous elephant. The elephant was so big and strong that everyone who saw it felt a mix of wonder and fear.

The king, with his large army and the giant elephant, began their journey toward Mecca. They planned to knock down the Kaaba, which was a very important and sacred place where people went to pray and feel close to God. As the army marched closer, the people of Mecca started to worry because they loved the Kaaba very much.

In Mecca, there lived a wise and kind man named Abdul Muttalib. He was known for his goodness and deep faith. Seeing the danger coming toward their beloved Kaaba, Abdul Muttalib prayed with all his heart, asking God to protect their sacred place. He believed that God would keep the Kaaba safe.

As the king's army approached Mecca, something amazing happened. When they got very close to the Kaaba, the huge elephant stopped walking. No matter how much the soldiers tried to make it move, it just wouldn't go forward toward the Kaaba. Instead, the elephant knelt down, as if it knew the place was too special to harm.

Right at that moment, the sky was filled with birds. Each bird carried small stones in their beaks and claws. These weren't just any birds; they seemed to be sent by God. They flew right over the king's army and began to drop the stones they were carrying. The stones fell with such force that the soldiers became scared and confused.

The stones kept coming, pelting the soldiers again and again. The powerful army was thrown into chaos, and the soldiers didn't know what to do. Facing such a strange and miraculous event, they realized they couldn't stay there any longer. Overwhelmed and frightened, they turned around and left, abandoning their plan to destroy the Kaaba.

The people of Mecca, who had been watching, were filled with awe and relief. They had seen a miracle happen right before their eyes! Their beloved Kaaba was safe, and they knew that their prayers had been answered. This event showed them how strong and powerful their faith was, and they were very thankful.

Abdul Muttalib and all the people in Mecca were overjoyed and filled with gratitude. They celebrated the protection of the Kaaba and praised God for the miracle. The story of the day the Kaaba was saved spread quickly and became known by everyone as the story of the "People of the Elephant."

The people of Mecca continued to take care of the Kaaba and welcomed travelers and pilgrims who came to visit the sacred place. The story of the People of the Elephant was told over and over, reminding everyone of the miraculous event that had protected their beloved Kaaba.

Moral of the Story:

This tale teaches us that faith and trust in goodness can lead to miraculous protections. It shows that when we believe in what is right and ask for help, amazing things can happen, helping us to overcome even the biggest challenges.

Chapter 15

The Two Sons of Adam

Once upon a time, long, long ago, there were two brothers named Cain and Abel. They were the very first brothers ever because their dad, Adam, was the first man in the world. Cain loved to grow fruits and vegetables in his garden. He was a farmer. Abel, the younger brother, loved to take care of animals. He was a shepherd and looked after his sheep with kindness.

Both brothers wanted to show they were thankful for what they had, so they decided to give some gifts to God. Abel picked the healthiest sheep from his flock because he wanted to give the very best. He chose a sheep that was strong, healthy, and beautiful. Abel cared deeply for his animals and wanted to show his gratitude to God by giving the best he had.

Cain, on the other hand, chose some fruits and veggies from his garden. But unlike Abel, Cain didn't choose the best of his crops. He picked some fruits and vegetables that were not as healthy or fresh. Cain gave his offering to God, but it wasn't from the heart like Abel's gift was.

God was very happy with Abel's gift because it was given from the heart. But God wasn't as pleased with Cain's offering because Cain didn't give his best. This made Cain feel very sad and also a bit angry with his brother. He thought it was unfair that God liked Abel's gift more.

Cain's feelings of anger and jealousy grew stronger every day. He tried to hide them, but it was hard. He didn't talk to anyone about how he felt, and his anger kept growing. One day, while they were in the field, Cain couldn't hold back his anger anymore. In a moment of great anger, he did something very bad to Abel. Sadly, Abel was hurt so badly he couldn't be fixed.

Right after this happened, Cain felt awful. He knew he had made a huge mistake. He was scared and didn't know what to do. God came to talk to Cain, asking, "Where is your brother Abel?" Cain, feeling scared and guilty, answered, "Am I supposed to keep track of my brother all the time?" But God already knew what had happened.

God was very sad about what Cain had done and told him that because of his actions, the ground wouldn't grow his plants well anymore. Cain's fields, which once grew plenty of fruits and vegetables, would now be barren and difficult to farm. And to help Cain remember this lesson and protect him from others who might be angry, God put a special mark on Cain's forehead. This mark was to show that Cain should not be harmed, despite his mistake.

Feeling very sorry, Cain left his home. He traveled to faraway places, always remembering the important lesson he had learned. The mark on his forehead reminded him every day to be better and to not let bad feelings lead him to make bad choices.

Wherever Cain went, people would learn about his story, and it helped them understand how important it is to handle feelings like anger and jealousy carefully. Cain met many people and shared his story, hoping others would learn from his mistake.

Moral of the Story:

This story helps us learn that being angry or jealous can lead to bad choices. It teaches us to be careful with our feelings and to always try to do what is right. We should also say sorry when we make mistakes and learn from them to become better people.

Chapter 16

Dhul-Qarnayn's Journey to Help

Once upon a time, in a land where the sun painted the desert sands gold every evening, there lived a wise and mighty king named Dhul-Qarnayn. Known for his strength, courage, and kindness, he ruled over a vast kingdom that reached into the far corners of the world. Dhul-Qarnayn was not only a ruler but also a great adventurer who loved to explore new lands and learn from different cultures.

One sunny morning, filled with the spirit of adventure, Dhul-Qarnayn gathered his closest friends and most loyal soldiers. He decided to embark on a grand journey to see the world beyond his kingdom. His heart swelled with excitement at the thought of discovering new places and meeting new people.

As they traveled, Dhul-Qarnayn and his companions crossed mighty rivers, climbed towering mountains, and trekked through bustling markets of distant cities. Everywhere he went, Dhul-Qarnayn showed great interest in the lives of the people he met, listening to their stories and learning about their ways of life.

One day, during their travels, Dhul-Qarnayn and his group came upon a peaceful valley. However, he quickly learned that this tranquility was threatened by raiders who often attacked the valley's villages. The people of the valley were kind and welcoming but lived in constant fear of these attacks.

Moved by their plight, Dhul-Qarnayn decided to help. He called upon his engineers and builders to construct a massive wall that would protect the valley. This wall would be made of iron and copper, materials strong enough to withstand any attack.

Finally, after many weeks of hard work, the great wall was completed. It stretched from one mountain to another, standing tall and strong against the landscape. The raiders, upon seeing the formidable barrier, knew they could no longer plunder the valley. Peace was restored to the land, and the people celebrated Dhul-Qarnayn's kindness and bravery.

But the king's journey did not end there. Dhul-Qarnayn continued to travel, reaching a place where the sun appeared to set into a dark, murky sea. He stood there, watching the sunset, and felt a deep sense of peace and wonder at the beauty of the world.

His next destination was a land scorched by the sun, where he found people suffering from the relentless heat. With compassion in his heart, Dhul-Qarnayn ordered the construction of a large shelter. It was built with tall pillars and a roof made of palm leaves, providing shade and comfort to the grateful people.

In another land, Dhul-Qarnayn met a group of people who were scared of wild animals attacking their homes. He instructed his soldiers to build strong fences around their village to keep the animals away. The villagers felt safe and protected, and they loved Dhul-Qarnayn for his help.

Throughout his travels, Dhul-Qarnayn spread peace and kindness, earning the love and respect of many. He returned home filled with unforgettable memories and stories, his heart full of joy from all the good he had done. The people of his kingdom welcomed him back with open arms, grateful for their wise and kind king.

Moral of the Story:

King Dhul-Qarnayn teaches us the importance of helping others. Through his journey, he showed that with courage, compassion, and determination, we can make the world a better place for everyone.

Chapter 17

The Story of Bravery and Belief

Once upon a time, in a beautiful land surrounded by green hills and big trees, there was a town filled with happy people. They liked to play in the sun and help each other. But there was one big problem: their king was very strict and unfair. He wanted everyone to think and act just like him and didn't let anyone have their own ideas.

The king, who had always lived in a big palace, was scared of any new ideas. He thought the only way to keep peace was for everyone to be just like him. So, the people of the town had to live by his strict rules, which made it hard for them to truly be happy or share their own thoughts.

One sunny morning, a wise man came to town. He was a kind traveler from a place far away and knew a lot about love and bravery. He gathered all the people in the center of the town and shared stories about a wonderful, caring Power that watched over everyone. He spoke about love, kindness, and standing up for what's right.

The people listened to the wise man and felt hope. His words were like tiny seeds of joy being planted in their hearts. They started meeting quietly to talk about these new ideas of love and caring for each other, which began to change the town.

But the king was not happy when he noticed these changes. He was very angry that the people were not following his rules anymore. So, he made a scary plan to stop them. He ordered his soldiers to dig a big ditch outside the town and fill it with fire. He told the people that anyone who wouldn't follow his rules would have to jump into the flames.

Everyone in town was scared when they heard this. They didn't want to give up their new beliefs but they were afraid of the fire. On the day they had to choose, they all came together. Among them was a young mother holding her little baby. As she walked close to the fiery ditch, she felt very scared but also strong inside. Suddenly, her baby, who had never spoken before, looked at her and said, "Be brave, mommy. We must do what is right."

This little miracle made everyone feel braver. They decided to be strong and not give in to the king's mean rule. They stood together, choosing kindness and love over fear.

Seeing this, the king realized he could not scare them into following him. The people's bravery and the wise man's words had changed the town forever. They had shown that even when you are scared, you can still choose to do what is right.

Moral of the Story:

Being brave means doing the right thing even when you are scared. This story teaches us that when we come together with love and bravery, we can change things for the better and never have to face challenges alone.

Chapter 18
Moses and Khidr's Adventures

Once upon a time, in a land of big deserts and wide rivers, there was a wise man named Moses. Moses knew a lot, but he always wanted to learn more.

One day, Moses decided to go on an adventure to find more wisdom. God told Moses to take a fish in a basket and follow it until it mysteriously disappeared. This would be the sign that he had found the person who would teach him new things. So, Moses took his fish and started walking with his young helper.

They walked over sandy hills and through the cool nights until they reached a place where two big seas met. They were tired and decided to rest. While they were resting, the fish slipped out of the basket and jumped into the sea, disappearing into the water. When Moses and his helper woke up and saw that the fish was gone, Moses knew this was the sign. They were in the right place!

Here, Moses met a man named Khidr. Moses asked Khidr if he could travel with him to learn new things. Khidr said yes, but he had one rule: "You must not ask about anything I do until I explain it to you," he said.

Moses agreed, and they started a strange and wonderful journey together. Their first stop was a small boat with poor fishermen. Khidr did something surprising—he made a hole in the boat! Moses forgot his promise and quickly asked, "Why did you do that?" Khidr reminded him that he shouldn't ask questions yet.

Next, they went to a village where nobody would give them food or a place to rest. The people there were not very friendly. There was a wall in the village that was about to fall down. Khidr fixed it with his own hands. Moses couldn't help but ask why Khidr helped people who were not kind to them. Again, Khidr reminded Moses about his promise.

After that, they traveled further and met a young boy playing. Khidr did something that shocked Moses—he hurt the boy. Moses was very upset and asked Khidr why he did such a thing. Khidr reminded him of his promise once more and told him this would be their last journey together because Moses could not keep from asking questions.

Finally, Khidr explained everything. The boat with the hole belonged to poor fishermen. There was a greedy king who would take any good boat he found. By making the hole, Khidr actually saved the boat from being taken by the king. The fishermen could fix the small hole and keep their boat.

The wall Khidr fixed was hiding a treasure meant for two orphans in the village. By fixing the wall, Khidr made sure the treasure stayed safe until the orphans were old enough to find it themselves.

As for the young boy, Khidr explained that the boy would grow up to be a very bad person and cause a lot of harm. By hurting him, Khidr prevented many future troubles for the boy's family and community.

Moses learned a lot that day. He learned that sometimes things that seem strange or even wrong can have good reasons behind them.

Moses thanked Khidr for the lessons and continued on his journey, now even wiser than before.

Moral of the Story:

This story teaches us that wisdom comes from experiencing life and learning that things aren't always what they seem at first. It teaches us patience and the importance of keeping an open mind.

Chapter 19

The Garden of Sharing

THE GARDEN OF SHARING

Once upon a time, in a sunny valley, there was a beautiful garden filled with the juiciest fruits and the prettiest flowers. This garden was so wonderful that everyone in the nearby village loved it. The garden was owned by a kind old man who loved to share. He always made sure that anyone who was hungry could come to his garden and eat the delicious fruits. No one ever left his garden hungry.

When the kind old man became very old, he knew he would soon leave the world. He called his three sons to his side and said, "This garden has given us much joy and fed many. Keep sharing its gifts with our village." The three sons promised to do so, remembering their father's love for sharing.

At first, the brothers kept their promise and shared the garden's fruits with the villagers. They enjoyed seeing the smiles on people's faces and hearing their words of thanks. But as time passed, the brothers began to think differently. "Why should we share all these fruits? If we keep them for ourselves, we could be the richest in the village," they thought. They made a secret plan to pick the fruits early in the morning before anyone could come.

The next morning, before the sun rose, the brothers went to the garden. It was still dark and cool. They walked quickly because they were eager to take all the fruits for themselves. But when they reached the garden, they were shocked. All the trees were bare! It looked as if no fruit had grown at all. They couldn't understand what had happened.

Feeling sad and confused, the brothers sat among the empty trees. They remembered their father's words about sharing and realized that being selfish was not making them happy at all. They felt sorry for trying to keep all the fruits to themselves.

The brothers decided to take care of the garden, hoping it might one day grow back. They watered the plants, pulled out the weeds, and made sure the soil was rich and healthy. They worked together, helping each other and the garden. Slowly, little green shoots started to appear. The garden was coming back to life!

The brothers were overjoyed and worked even harder to take care of the new plants. As the garden grew back, they made sure to share the new fruits with everyone. They noticed that the more they shared, the happier they felt. The garden flourished even more than before, filled with laughter and joy from all who visited.

The brothers learned an important lesson from this. They saw that the garden was happiest when its fruits were shared. From then on, they never forgot to share everything the garden offered. They realized that sharing brought more happiness and prosperity to everyone, including themselves.

Moral of the Story:

Sharing brings joy not just to others, but to ourselves too. The brothers learned that happiness grows when we share what we have, just like the fruits in their garden.

Chapter 20

The Rich Man's Lesson

Once upon a time, in a land full of rolling hills and sparkling rivers, there were two friends. One friend was very rich and owned two big, beautiful gardens. These gardens were like paradise on earth, filled with the most colorful flowers and the juiciest fruits anyone had ever tasted. Little streams of cool water flowed between the trees, making the air fresh and sweet. Birds loved these gardens too; they sang their beautiful songs from morning till night.

The rich man, who owned these gardens, felt very proud of what he had. One sunny day, as he walked through his gardens with his friend, he couldn't help but boast. "Look at my wonderful gardens! I have so much, and I'm sure I will never lose it. I'm richer than many, and I don't think even the end of the world could take this wealth from me!" he said loudly.

His friend, who wasn't as rich but was very wise, listened quietly to all this boasting. He felt a bit sad because he knew that everything in life is a gift and should be appreciated with a humble heart. The wise friend believed in being thankful for every blessing.

As they continued to walk, the rich man kept boasting. "I will never have problems," he claimed. "And even if problems come, I have enough money to solve them all!"

The wise friend tried to give some gentle advice. "My dear friend," he said, "it's better to be humble and always say 'God willing' when you talk about the future. We should be thankful for what we have today because it can all disappear tomorrow."

But the rich man just laughed and didn't listen to his friend's wise words.

Not long after their conversation, a huge storm hit the valley. It was a terrible storm with loud thunder, bright lightning, and very heavy rain. The rivers that once gently flowed through the gardens swelled up quickly and flooded everything. The flood was so strong that it destroyed everything in the gardens.

When the storm finally passed, the rich man rushed to see his gardens. He was shocked to find that his beautiful paradise was gone. The trees were uprooted, the flowers were washed away, and all the fruits were destroyed. His beautiful gardens were now just mud and debris.

The rich man was very sad. He remembered what his wise friend had told him about being humble and grateful. He realized how wrong he had been to boast and feel so secure in his wealth.

He went to find his friend and said, "You were right. I was so foolish not to listen to your wise words. Now, I see how quickly things can change. From now on, I will always be grateful and remember to say 'God willing' when I talk about what I have."

The rich man learned a valuable lesson about humility and gratitude. He worked hard to rebuild his gardens, but this time, he made sure to share the beauty and fruits with everyone in the village. He became known not only for his gardens but also for his kindness and generosity. The rich man's heart had changed, and he found joy in sharing and being grateful for each day.

Moral of the Story:

We should always be thankful and humble about our blessings. Sharing what we have brings true happiness and keeps us prepared for the changes life may bring.

Chapter 21

Solomon and the Tiny Teachers

Once upon a time, in a land filled with sand dunes and lush oases, there lived a wise king named Solomon. King Solomon was no ordinary king; he had a very special gift. He could understand and talk to animals and insects! Yes, from the mighty lions to the tiny ants, he could hear what they were saying and speak with them.

One sunny day, King Solomon decided to take a long walk with his large army. They marched with great pride, their armor gleaming under the bright sun, and their spirits high with joy. As they passed through a vast desert, they approached a valley where hundreds of ants were busy at work.

In this valley lived an ant queen who was very wise and caring. She watched over her colony like a good queen should. As King Solomon's grand army neared, the ground trembled with the weight of the marching soldiers. The tiny ants felt the ground shake and were worried that they might get stepped on.

The ant queen, seeing the approaching danger, quickly warned her fellow ants. "Hurry, my friends!" she cried. "Run to your homes! A great army is coming, and we don't want to be in their way. They might not see us, and we could get hurt!"

Her voice was so soft and gentle, yet it carried strongly to all her ant friends. All the ants listened to their queen and scurried towards their tiny holes, carrying the food they had gathered. They moved quickly and efficiently, all thanks to their queen's timely warning.

Now, King Solomon, with his special gift, heard what the ant queen had said. He was deeply touched by her concern for her tiny subjects. He realized that even though his army was mighty, they had to be careful not to harm even the smallest creature like an ant.

With a warm heart and a wise mind, King Solomon ordered his entire army to stop. He then directed them to take another path, one that would not disturb the ants' home. "Let us be mindful of all creatures," he told his soldiers. "Each creature is important and deserves our respect and care."

The soldiers obeyed King Solomon's orders and carefully changed their route. The ants watched in relief as the huge feet of soldiers moved away from their homes, leaving them safe. The tiny ants cheered for their queen who had saved them and also felt grateful for the kind king who had listened.

From that day on, King Solomon paid even closer attention to all the creatures of the land. And so, King Solomon grew wiser each day because he understood that wisdom isn't just about great deeds or wise sayings; it's about showing kindness and consideration to everyone—no matter how big or how small.

Moral of the Story:

This story teaches us about empathy, respect for all living beings, and how wisdom can often come from the most unexpected places.

Chapter 22

Prophet Hud and the Windy City

Once upon a time, in a huge desert with giant sand dunes, there was a city called 'Ad. This city was famous because the people living there were super strong and they built very tall buildings that almost touched the sky. The people of 'Ad were very proud of their buildings and their strength.

In 'Ad, there lived a kind and wise man named Prophet Hud. He was sent by God to help and guide the people. Prophet Hud noticed that the people were not being grateful for what they had. They always bragged about their buildings and how strong they were, but they forgot to be thankful and did not care for each other properly.

Prophet Hud tried to help them. He said, "Why don't you thank God for all your strength and beautiful buildings? It's great to be strong and to have such a wonderful city, but it's also important to be kind and help each other." But the people just laughed at him. They did not listen because they thought they did not need any help.

Prophet Hud did not give up. For many years, he told them beautiful stories about being kind, talked about how important it was to be thankful, and showed them ways to look after one another. However, the people of 'Ad kept ignoring his advice. They continued being proud and forgot about being kind and grateful.

Then, one day, dark clouds covered the sky over 'Ad. A very strong wind started to blow. At first, the people were not worried. They believed their strong buildings would protect them from any storm. But this was no ordinary storm; the wind was much stronger than anything they had ever seen.

Prophet Hud came to them again, saying, "Please, let's ask for forgiveness and learn to respect and care for what we have and each other." But even with the howling winds outside, the people's hearts were still hard. They did not listen to him.

The storm lasted for seven nights and eight days. It was so powerful that it destroyed all the tall buildings. The mighty city that once stood proudly was now in ruins. The very strong buildings they thought could withstand anything were gone.

During the storm, Prophet Hud and a few people who believed his words gathered together. They stayed inside a small, sturdy house that Prophet Hud had built with care and wisdom. The strong wind howled outside, but they were safe inside, praying and hoping for the storm to end.

After the storm passed, the sun finally came out. The sky was clear again, but the city of 'Ad was in ruins. The tall buildings were broken, and the streets were filled with debris. The people who had laughed at Prophet Hud and ignored his advice were gone.

Prophet Hud and the few believers who had survived the storm looked at the destruction around them. They knew they had been saved because they had listened to Prophet Hud and learned to be kind, thankful, and respectful. They decided to leave the ruined city and find a new place to live.

They traveled for many days through the desert until they found a beautiful valley with green fields and fresh water. They decided to build a new city there. This time, they remembered the lessons Prophet Hud had taught them. They worked together, helped each other, and always remembered to be grateful for what they had.

Moral of the Story:

Kindness, gratitude, and respect are powerful. Even when big problems come, these qualities can help us stand strong and rebuild.

Chapter 23

The Marvelous Camel of Salih

Long ago, in a land surrounded by rocky mountains and vast deserts, there was a town called Thamud. The people of Thamud were very skilled and could carve beautiful homes directly from the mountainsides. They were strong, proud, and smart.

Among them was a wise and kind man named Prophet Salih. Everyone loved him for his kindness and the wise things he taught. Prophet Salih was chosen by God to help the people of Thamud live better lives by being thankful, respecting each other, and caring for nature.

One day, Prophet Salih gathered everyone in the town square. He had something important to share. He stood before the crowd and said, "My dear friends, we are lucky to have many blessings, but we must remember to be thankful and not be greedy. We need to look after our land and each other."

However, some people in the town didn't believe Salih's words. They wanted proof that he was really sent by God. They asked for a miracle, something amazing that they had never seen before.

Prophet Salih prayed, and a wonderful thing happened—a huge, beautiful camel appeared from the mountains. This camel was a gift from God. It was very strong and provided enough milk for everyone in the town.

Prophet Salih told the people, "This camel is a gift for all of us, but we must take good care of it and share it. It should be allowed to drink from our well every other day." Everyone was amazed by the camel, but not everyone was pleased.

As time went on, the camel became a normal part of their lives. The children loved to watch the camel, and the people enjoyed the fresh milk it provided. However, a few people became greedy. They didn't want to share the water or the milk. These greedy few made a plan to get rid of the camel so they could have all the resources for themselves.

One sad day, they went ahead with their plan and hurt the miraculous camel. When Prophet Salih found out, he was very upset. He warned them that their selfish act would have serious consequences.

Three days later, just as Salih had warned, a terrible earthquake shook the town. The beautiful homes carved into the mountains were destroyed. The ground rumbled and shook, and the people ran in fear. Only those who had respected the camel and lived as Prophet Salih advised were saved.

The earthquake was a tough lesson for the people of Thamud. They realized that their greed and selfishness had led to their downfall. The survivors left the town, promising to live differently and remember the lessons they learned from Prophet Salih and the marvelous camel.

They traveled to a new land, where they built new homes and communities. This time, they made sure to take care of each other and their resources. They shared their blessings and remembered to be thankful for everything they had.

Moral of the Story:

We must cherish and protect the shared blessings in our lives. Being greedy and selfish can harm everyone in our community, but gratitude and respect can make our world a better place.

Chapter 24

The Garden of Greed

THE GARDEN OF GREED

Once upon a time, in a sunny valley surrounded by tall mountains and sparkling rivers, there lived two men. One man was very rich and had a large, beautiful garden. This garden was filled with the sweetest fruits and the most colorful flowers you could imagine. The other man was very poor, owning only a small patch of land, just big enough to grow vegetables for his family.

The rich man loved to walk through his garden. He enjoyed looking at the trees heavy with fruit and the rows of bright flowers. He felt very proud of all he owned and liked to show off his garden to his friends.

One day, the rich man decided to throw a big party. He invited all the rich people from nearby towns. Everyone who came couldn't stop talking about how wonderful his garden was. This made the rich man feel even prouder and more pleased with himself.

Nearby, the poor man lived in a small, simple house. He didn't have much, but he was generous and kind. He always shared whatever he had with others. His home was filled with laughter and joy, even though the meals were simple.

The rich man noticed how happy the poor man seemed and wondered, "How can he be so happy when he has so little?" So, one day, he asked the poor man, "Why are you so content when you have almost nothing?"

The poor man smiled and answered, "I don't have much money or many things, but I have enough. My family is happy, and we share what we have. That makes us feel good."

The rich man couldn't understand this. He thought having more money and more things was the secret to happiness. So, he kept adding more trees and more flowers to his garden, hoping to become happier.

But then, a big storm came to the valley. The storm was very strong, and it damaged the rich man's garden badly. Many trees fell down, and the beautiful flowers were ruined. The rich man was very sad to see his once beautiful garden destroyed.

Walking through the damaged garden, he remembered what the poor man had said about happiness. He realized that maybe there was another way to find joy.

Feeling that he needed to change, the rich man went to visit the poor man. He started helping him in his small garden and learned how to care for others. Over time, they became good friends, and the rich man discovered the joy of sharing and being kind.

The rich man decided to fix his garden but made a change. He turned it into a place where everyone in the valley could come and enjoy the fruits and flowers. He shared everything he grew with others, and soon, he found that this made him happier than he had ever been.

From that day on, the rich man and the poor man remained good friends. They worked together to keep the garden beautiful and to help others in the valley. The rich man never forgot the lesson he had learned: that true happiness comes from sharing and caring for others.

Moral of the Story:

Happiness doesn't come from what we have but from what we share. By giving to others, we find true joy and make our lives richer and more meaningful.

Chapter 25

Shuaib and the Town of Madyan

Long ago, in a lively town called Madyan, nestled between lush green hills and sparkling streams, there was a busy market known to all. Traders from nearby and far-off places came to sell their wares. But there was a big problem in Madyan: many of the town's traders were not honest. Instead of being fair, they would trick their customers by giving them less than what they paid for.

Prophet Shuaib was really upset about the unfairness in the market. He believed that being fair made everyone happier and made Madyan a stronger, better place.

One bright morning, under the warm sun, Prophet Shuaib went to the middle of the market. He gathered the people around and spoke with a gentle but firm voice, "My dear friends, why do you cheat with your scales? When you give less than what others have paid for, you might think it makes you richer today, but it will hurt us all in the end."

Some traders paused to listen, but many just laughed and carried on with their dishonest ways. They liked the extra money from cheating and didn't care much about being fair.

But Prophet Shuaib didn't lose hope. Every day, he would return to the market and talk about the importance of honesty. He explained,

"Some of you think you're getting richer by being dishonest, but real wealth comes from trust and respect, not cheating."

As time went by, a few people started to listen to Prophet Shuaib. They noticed how everyone respected him for his fair dealings, and they began to change. They started trading honestly, measuring things accurately, and treating everyone kindly.

One day, a young boy named Sami, who helped his father in the market, heard Prophet Shuaib's words. Sami was curious and wanted to know more. He asked Prophet Shuaib, "Why is being honest so important?"

Prophet Shuaib smiled and said, "When we are honest, people trust us. Trust is like a strong bridge that connects us with others. Without it, everything falls apart. Honest trading brings blessings and happiness to everyone."

Sami thought about this and decided to always be honest in his dealings. He made sure to measure the goods fairly and never cheat the customers. People soon began to notice Sami's honesty, and more customers came to his father's stall.

However, many traders still refused to change their ways. They thought Prophet Shuaib's ideas were old-fashioned and believed cheating was easier.

Then one day, something dramatic happened—a huge earthquake shook Madyan. It was very scary, and the buildings of those who had been dishonest crumbled to the ground, while the homes of fair traders stood strong. It seemed as if the very land was upset with the dishonest traders.

After the earthquake, the people of Madyan saw that Prophet Shuaib had been right all along. Those who survived came together to rebuild their town. This time, they built it on the principles of honesty and trust. They remembered all that Prophet Shuaib had taught them, and these lessons were passed down through the generations.

Moral of the Story:

A community built on honesty and trust not only brings prosperity but also stands strong against challenges. Being fair and truthful brings true wealth and happiness.

Chapter 26

King Solomon's Missing Advisor

Long ago, in a land where palm trees danced in the wind and vast deserts spread far and wide, there lived a king named Solomon. This king was no ordinary ruler; he was wise and had a very special gift—he could talk to animals and even understand the whispers of the wind.

One sunny morning, as King Solomon held his daily court, he noticed something odd. His trusted advisor, who was usually by his side, was missing. This advisor was very loyal and never missed a day of court. As days went by without any sign of him, King Solomon grew worried.

Determined to find out what had happened to his advisor, King Solomon wandered through his vast gardens, thinking deeply. It was during this walk that he overheard a conversation that caught his attention. It was a group of ants, chattering about a strange sight they had seen in a hidden corner of the garden—a place rarely visited by anyone.

Filled with curiosity, King Solomon decided to follow the tiny ants. They led him along narrow paths, under blooming flowers, and through thick bushes. Finally, they reached a secluded spot where he found a staff leaning against a tree. Next to it, his missing advisor was lying peacefully as if he were asleep.

Upon closer inspection, King Solomon realized that his advisor had passed away. This discovery saddened King Solomon deeply, but it also taught him something important about life and duty.

King Solomon learned that life is fragile and can end unnoticed like that of his silent, loyal advisor standing in the garden. He was grateful to the tiny ants for leading him to this discovery and solving the mystery of his missing friend.

He returned to his palace, his heart heavy with the lesson he had learned. He shared this experience with his people, telling them about his advisor's dedication and the ants' helpfulness. King Solomon emphasized how even the smallest creatures could provide wisdom and how important it is to appreciate everyone's role, no matter how big or small.

King Solomon continued to pay attention to all the creatures in his kingdom. One day, as he was walking in his garden, he saw a line of ants carrying food back to their nest. He marveled at their teamwork and how each ant played its part in helping the colony. He knelt down and spoke to the ants, thanking them for their hard work and reminding them of the valuable lesson they had taught him.

The ants were pleased to have helped the wise king and continued their work with renewed energy. King Solomon watched them for a while, reflecting on the importance of every creature in his kingdom. He realized that everyone, no matter how small, had a role to play and that their contributions were essential to the well-being of the whole kingdom.

And so, King Solomon ruled his kingdom with kindness and wisdom, always remembering the lesson he learned from the ants and his loyal advisor.

Moral of the Story:

Every creature, no matter how small, has value and can teach us important lessons. By listening to the smallest voices, we can learn to appreciate and cherish every moment and every life.

Chapter 27

Moses and the Wise Fisherman

Once upon a time, in a land of rolling hills and sparkling rivers, there lived a great prophet named Moses. Moses was chosen by God to guide people and teach them important lessons about life. One sunny day, while walking through a picturesque village, Moses met a humble fisherman sitting by a river.

The fisherman, spotting Moses, waved and called him over. "Hello, Prophet Moses! Would you like to sit with me for a while?" he asked kindly. Moses accepted the invitation and sat down beside the fisherman who was preparing his fishing rod.

As they sat quietly by the river, the fisherman cast his line into the glistening water and waited patiently. The line floated peacefully on the surface. Moses watched and admired the calm and patient manner of the fisherman.

After some time, the fisherman turned to Moses and shared a thought. "You know, Prophet Moses, I've learned that being patient is very important in fishing. We must wait calmly and trust that the fish will come when they are ready," he explained.

Moses listened carefully and thought about the fisherman's words. He realized there was a deep lesson in patience here. He reflected on the times when he had been in a hurry or wanted things to happen quickly without giving them the time they needed.

Their peaceful silence was broken by a gentle tug on the fishing line. The fisherman reacted swiftly, pulling up a beautiful, shimmering fish. He smiled at his catch but then did something surprising. He gently removed the hook and released the fish back into the river.

"I catch fish not just to keep them but to enjoy the moment and learn from nature," the fisherman said with a smile. "Releasing them back is my way of showing respect for the life of every creature."

Moses was moved by the fisherman's respect for nature. He learned how every action, even a simple one like fishing, could show kindness and consideration for all living things.

As the sun began to set, casting a warm glow over the water, Moses and the fisherman continued to talk. The fisherman shared stories about his life by the river. He talked about the changing seasons, the animals he saw, and the lessons he learned from watching the world around him.

Moses listened intently, feeling a sense of peace and understanding growing within him. He realized that wisdom could be found in the simplest of places and that everyone, no matter how humble, had something valuable to teach.

Before they parted ways, the fisherman said, "Remember, Prophet Moses, every moment teaches us something important if we are willing to learn." Moses thanked the fisherman for his wisdom and continued on his way, feeling enlightened.

As Moses walked back to his village, he noticed the beauty of the world around him with new eyes. The rustling of the leaves, the songs of the birds, and the gentle flow of the river all seemed to hold important lessons. He thought about how patience, respect, and kindness could bring harmony to life.

Moral of the Story:

Patience, respect, and kindness teach us valuable lessons and bring harmony to our lives. Even simple acts can reflect deep respect for life and nature, enriching our understanding and appreciation of the world around us.

Chapter 28

Abraham and the Broken Idols

In a land of golden sands and starry skies, there was a kind man named Abraham. He lived in a busy town where many people believed in different gods. They made statues from stone and wood and thought these statues had special powers.

Abraham was different. He didn't believe these statues could do anything because they were made by people. He believed in one true God who created the stars, the earth, and everything on it. This belief made Abraham feel peaceful and strong.

Every day, Abraham saw his neighbors praying to their statues. They gave gifts to the statues, hoping to get something good in return. This made Abraham very sad. He knew these statues couldn't see or hear or do anything.

One day, Abraham decided to show the people they were mistaken. He waited until everyone was asleep and went quietly into the place where all the statues were kept. With a hammer in his hand and courage in his heart, Abraham knocked over all the statues except for the biggest one. He left the hammer next to it.

The next morning, when people came to pray, they found all their statues broken. They were very upset and confused. "Who did this?" they asked each other in shock.

Abraham stepped forward. He was calm and not afraid. "Maybe the big statue did it," he suggested. "Why don't you ask him?"

The people looked at the big statue, then at the hammer, and then at each other. They knew the statue couldn't do anything—it was just a big piece of stone. Abraham's words started to make sense to them. They realized their statues couldn't see, hear, or help anyone because they were just objects.

After this, some of the townspeople began to think differently. They remembered Abraham's words about the one true God who wasn't made of stone or wood. Slowly, more and more people stopped believing in the statues and started to share Abraham's belief in one God.

Abraham taught them that this God didn't need gifts of food or gold. He wanted people to live with kindness and respect for each other. With this new understanding, the town became a peaceful place, where neighbors cared more about each other's happiness than about pleasing statues.

As time went on, Abraham continued to share his beliefs and show kindness to everyone, whether they agreed with him or not. He spoke to them gently and answered their questions with patience. He told them stories about the beauty of the world and the wonders of nature, all created by the one true God.

The people began to see the truth in Abraham's words. They noticed that the sun rose and set each day, the stars twinkled at night, and the rain brought life to their crops—all without the help of their statues. They started to appreciate the world around them and understand that their true blessings came from the one God Abraham spoke of.

Moral of the Story:

True belief comes from understanding and feeling, not from objects we can see or touch. Abraham's story teaches us that questioning and seeking the truth can lead us to greater understanding and peace.

Chapter 29

The Miracles of Prophet Elisha

In a village surrounded by lush green fields and colorful flowers, there lived a kind man named Elisha. Elisha was special because he was a prophet, chosen by God to help people.

Elisha was famous for performing miracles that brought happiness and hope to those in need. His heart was so full of love that he couldn't help but share it with everyone around him.

One sunny morning, a woman from the village came to see Elisha. She looked very sad. Her husband had passed away, and she was left with two young sons and a big debt she couldn't pay. She was worried and didn't know what to do.

Seeing her sadness, Elisha felt a strong wish to help her. He knew that with God's help, he could find a way to make things better. He asked the woman, "What do you have in your house?"

The woman replied, "I have nothing at all except a small jar of oil."

Elisha smiled gently and said, "Go and ask your neighbors for empty jars. Don't just ask for a few, ask for many. Then go inside your house with your sons and shut the door. Pour oil into all the jars, and as each is filled, put it to one side."

The woman did as Elisha had told her. She and her sons gathered many empty jars from their neighbors. They went inside their house and shut the door. She began to pour oil from her small jar into the empty ones. To her amazement, the oil kept flowing until all the jars were full.

The woman returned to Elisha and told him what had happened. He said, "Go, sell the oil and pay your debts. You and your sons can live on what is left." The woman was overjoyed. Her problem was solved, and she was very grateful to Elisha.

News of Elisha's kindness and the amazing miracles he performed spread across the village and even to places far away. People came from all over to seek his help, bringing their problems and pains to him.

One of these people was a man who had lost his sight and could no longer see. He heard about Elisha and, with hope in his heart, came to ask for help. Elisha felt deep compassion for him. He gently touched the man's eyes and prayed.

Miraculously, the man's sight returned. He opened his eyes and could see everything clearly again. He was overjoyed and thanked Elisha, tears of happiness rolling down his cheeks.

Another time, a group of people came to Elisha with a very serious problem. Their land had become barren, and their crops were failing because the water in their river had turned bad. It was undrinkable and made their fields dry.

Elisha went with the people to the river. He took a little salt and threw it into the water, praying to God to make the water clean again. As soon as he did this, the water became pure and fresh. The people were amazed and happy that their river was restored. They could now drink the water and their crops would grow again.

Elisha's life was filled with acts of kindness, and he showed everyone that with a little faith, great things are possible.

Moral of the Story:

Helping others is one of the most powerful ways to spread happiness. Elisha's story teaches us that kindness and caring are very important, and by helping others, we can make the world a better place.

Chapter 30

Prophet Muhammad's Adventure

Once upon a time in the city of Mecca, there lived a very kind and humble man named Muhammad. Muhammad was not just any man; he was a prophet chosen by God to bring messages of love, peace, and unity to everyone.

One special night, something amazing happened. As Muhammad was sleeping, he was visited by the angel Gabriel. The angel woke him up gently and took him outside where a magnificent winged creature named Buraq waited. This was no ordinary night; it was the beginning of a wondrous journey through the heavens.

Buraq soared into the sky with Muhammad, climbing higher and higher. They flew past twinkling stars and slid across the Milky Way until they reached a magical place called the Farthest Mosque, also known as Al-Aqsa Mosque in Jerusalem. Here, Muhammad saw something incredible—prophets from the past, all together, praying in peace and unity.

Their journey didn't stop there. Muhammad and the angel Gabriel continued their journey through seven different heavens. Each heaven was more beautiful than the last, filled with angels and secrets of the universe that Muhammad had never known. He met prophets such as Adam, Jesus, and Moses, and he learned about the wonders of creation and the vastness of the cosmos.

At the very top of the heavens, Muhammad experienced something extraordinary. He felt the presence of God. It was a moment of pure awe, filled with peace and enlightenment. This special encounter filled his heart with immense joy and gratitude. God gave Muhammad important instructions and messages for his followers.

After this miraculous adventure through the skies, Muhammad returned to Mecca. He couldn't wait to tell everyone about his journey. He shared all the amazing things he had seen and the deep wisdom he had received. He talked about the unity of the prophets, the beauty of the heavens, and the love and guidance he felt from God.

The people of Mecca listened with wide eyes and open hearts. They were amazed by Muhammad's stories and inspired by his strong faith and courage. He had seen things they could hardly imagine, and his unwavering belief in God's power and kindness touched everyone.

Muhammad's incredible journey taught his followers many things. He showed them that faith is powerful and that perseverance and trust in God can lead to extraordinary experiences. He reminded them that there is always light and guidance available, even on the darkest nights, for those who seek it with sincere hearts.

Muhammad continued to spread his message, helping his followers to understand the importance of being together in faith and love. He encouraged them to always seek knowledge, to be open to the mysteries of life, and to strive for goodness and unity among all people.

The story of Muhammad's journey, known as the Isra and Mi'raj, became a cherished tale that people shared with their children and grandchildren. It inspired everyone to believe in the power of faith and the importance of seeking wisdom and understanding.

Moral of the Story:

Muhammad's journey teaches us that faith and openness can lead to miraculous experiences. We learn that seeking understanding and being united in love and peace are important steps toward living a fulfilled and enlightened life.

Chapter 31

Moses and the Talking Stone

Once upon a time, in a beautiful land with rolling hills and flowing rivers, there lived a wise and kind man named Moses. Moses was a special man, chosen by God to guide his people and teach them about faith and doing what is right.

One hot day, Moses was traveling with his people through a dry, sandy desert. Everyone was tired, hot, and very thirsty. They needed water to drink, but there was none to be found. The people came to Moses, worried and asking for help to find water in the vast desert.

Moses knew they needed a miracle, so he turned to God for help. With strong faith and hope in his heart, he prayed for water to quench their thirst. After his prayer, God told Moses to use his staff to strike a large stone nearby.

Gathering his people around the stone, Moses raised his staff and struck the stone as God had instructed. Suddenly, to everyone's amazement, water started to gush out from the stone! It poured out like a beautiful, clear stream, and all the people rushed to drink from it, filling their cups with the cool, refreshing water.

But something even more incredible happened next. As the people drank happily, the stone itself began to speak! It had a gentle and wise voice, and it began to thank Moses for freeing the water and praised God for His kindness and generosity.

The people listened in wonder as the stone spoke about how important it is to have faith, to be thankful, and to trust in God's help. The talking stone reminded them that even during tough times, God's blessings are always close by, ready to help those who believe and ask for guidance.

Moses and his followers felt a new strength after hearing the stone's wise words. They continued their journey through the desert, feeling grateful and reassured. They remembered the talking stone and the miracle of the water, and it helped them to keep going.

As they walked, Moses shared more about what the miracle meant. He explained that God's blessings could come in surprising ways and that even simple things like a stone could show God's love and care.

Years later, when the people reached their promised land, they built a small monument to remember the talking stone. It became a place where they gathered to give thanks and to teach their children about faith and God's miracles.

The story of Moses and the talking stone was passed down through generations, reminding everyone of the power of faith, gratitude, and the unexpected ways blessings can come into their lives.

Moral of the Story:

Miracles happen when we have faith and trust in God. The story of Moses and the talking stone teaches us to appreciate the unexpected ways blessings come into our lives and to always be grateful for the gifts we receive.

Chapter 32

Prophet Elias and the Fire

In a beautiful land filled with green valleys and high mountains, there was a wise man named Elias. Elias was not just any man; he was a prophet, chosen by God to help guide the people in his village and teach them important lessons.

Elias lived in a time when many people in his village had forgotten to worship God. Instead, they worshipped statues made from stone and wood, believing these idols could bring them good luck and happiness. Elias knew this wasn't right, and he wanted to help the people understand and return to worshipping God.

One day, Elias called all the villagers to come to a large open field at the foot of the mountains. He wanted to show them something important. "Today, we will have a test to see who can truly bring us help and blessings," Elias announced to the curious crowd.

The villagers who worshipped idols were asked to set up a big pile of wood and pray to their idols to set it on fire. They agreed and started praying loudly, hoping for a fire. They chanted and waited eagerly, but nothing happened. The wood just sat there, cold and untouched.

The villagers prayed harder and even danced around the woodpile, trying everything they could think of to get their idols to set the wood on fire. They waited and waited, but still, nothing happened. The people began to feel worried and confused.

Then it was Elias's turn. He quietly set up his own pile of wood. Instead of shouting or dancing, Elias simply prayed to God in a calm and sincere voice, asking for help to show the truth to his people.

As soon as Elias finished his prayer, something amazing happened. A bolt of lightning flashed across the sky and struck the wood, setting it ablaze with a warm, bright fire. The villagers gasped and watched in awe as the flames danced under the sky.

Seeing this miracle, the people were amazed and began to understand Elias's message. They realized that the statues they had been praying to couldn't do anything, while Elias's prayer to God was answered right away.

After this event, many villagers started to change their ways. They listened to Elias as he taught them more about God's love and how to live lives filled with kindness, truth, and respect for one another.

One day, a little boy named Sam came to Elias with a question. "Prophet Elias, how can we show our love for God every day?" Elias smiled and said, "By being kind to each other, helping those in need, and always being honest. These are ways to show our love and respect for God."

The villagers took Elias's words to heart. They began to help each other more, sharing their food and taking care of those who were sick or in need. The village became a place of love and kindness, where everyone felt welcome and cared for.

The people thanked Elias for helping them find their way back to faith, and they worked together to build a community that cared for every person and lived gratefully under God's guidance.

Moral of the Story:

The story of Prophet Elias teaches us about the power of true faith and the importance of following what is right. Elias showed his people that real miracles happen when we believe in God and live by His teachings, reminding us to always seek truth and kindness in our lives.

Chapter 33

The Day the Sun Stood Still

In a land filled with lush green plains and abundant orchards, there lived a wise and patient man named Prophet Yusha'. Yusha' was not an ordinary man; he was a chosen prophet, blessed with divine wisdom to lead his people on a path of righteousness and faith.

One bright morning, Yusha' was guiding his followers through a vast, sun-baked desert. They had been walking for days, and everyone was tired and thirsty. Finally, they saw something ahead—a wide, swift-flowing river. The river was blocking their way to the safe lands beyond. The water rushed and roared, making it impossible for anyone to cross.

The people were worried. "How will we get across?" they asked. Yusha', calm and filled with faith, knew that they needed a miracle. He lifted his hands towards the heavens and prayed earnestly for assistance. He called upon God to part the waters of the river so that his people could safely reach the other side.

As Yusha' concluded his prayers, a breathtaking miracle unfolded before their eyes. The waters of the river slowly started to pull back, parting down the middle and revealing a dry, sandy path. The people were amazed and filled with gratitude as they walked across the riverbed, their feet stirring up clouds of dust where water had just been.

The people cheered and hugged each other as they reached the other side. They were safe and felt blessed by the miracle they had just witnessed. But their journey was not over. As they ventured further, they soon faced another challenge—a mighty army that threatened to harm them and block their path to the promised safety.

Once again, Yusha' turned to God for help. He prayed for protection and guidance against the formidable foes that lay ahead. Responding to his faith, a second miracle occurred: the sun, which had been rapidly descending towards the horizon, slowed its pace, bathing the battlefield in a prolonged golden light.

This divine intervention allowed Yusha' and his followers to clearly see their adversaries. Empowered and emboldened, they managed to fend off the enemy with renewed strength and courage. Time seemed to stand still as the sun delayed its setting, extending the day until they had secured a victorious outcome.

As darkness finally fell and the battle ceased, Yusha' and his people celebrated their triumph. They knew deeply that it was through God's mercy and guidance that they had overcome their challenges.

From that day on, Yusha' and his followers continued their journey, strengthened by the memory of the miraculous events they had witnessed. Their hearts were filled with unshakable faith and a deep understanding that no obstacle was too great when supported by divine grace.

They faced many more challenges, but each time, they remembered Yusha's teachings and the miracles they had experienced. With faith and determination, they overcame every obstacle in their path.

Finally, after many days of travel, they reached the promised land. It was a beautiful place with fertile soil, clear streams, and plenty of food. The people were overjoyed and thanked Yusha' for his guidance and leadership.

Moral of the Story:

With faith, patience, and trust in God, even the most daunting obstacles can be overcome. God's guidance ensures that with perseverance, we can emerge victorious from adversity.

Chapter 34

Prophet Zakariya and John

In a small, peaceful town filled with colorful gardens and sweet-smelling flowers, there lived a kind and gentle man named Zakariya. Zakariya wasn't just any townsman; he was a chosen prophet of God. He was known all around for his deep devotion to prayer and his unwavering belief in God's goodness.

Zakariya shared his life with his wife, Elizabeth, who was just as faithful and good-hearted as he was. Together, they had one wish that they held close to their hearts—they longed to have a child who would fill their home with laughter and happiness. But as the years went by, they both grew older, and it seemed more and more unlikely that their wish would come true.

Then, one very special day, while Zakariya was praying alone in a quiet sanctuary, something miraculous happened. The angel Gabriel appeared before him with a joyous message directly from God. The angel told Zakariya that he would soon have a son named John. This son would grow up to be a great prophet, sharing God's words and bringing joy to many.

Zakariya was overjoyed and filled with gratitude, but a tiny part of him wondered how such a thing could happen, especially since they were both so old. Despite his doubts, he thanked God for this wonderful promise.

Not long after Gabriel's visit, Elizabeth found out she was going to have a baby. The news filled their home with excitement and happiness. It was clear that God had listened to their prayers and was fulfilling His promise.

The day John was born was one of the happiest days of Zakariya and Elizabeth's lives. They named him John, just as the angel had said. As John grew, it was obvious he was no ordinary child. He was wise, kind, and deeply connected to God. He respected his parents and followed his father's teachings closely.

John had a special way of talking to people. He made friends easily and always knew the right things to say to make others feel better. He loved helping people and often shared his food with those who were hungry. Zakariya and Elizabeth watched with pride as their son grew up to be a kind and gentle young man.

As John got older, he felt a strong calling to share God's messages with everyone. He became known as John the Baptist. He traveled around, talking to people about living good lives, being kind to each other, and following God's path. He became very respected and loved, teaching about the importance of being humble and helping others.

John would stand by the river and speak to crowds of people. He would tell them about God's love and how they should live their lives with honesty and kindness. People listened to him and felt inspired to be better.

Years passed, and John's teachings continued to inspire many. Zakariya and Elizabeth lived long enough to see their son become a beacon of hope and faith for countless people. They knew that God's promise had brought more joy and fulfillment into their lives than they had ever imagined.

Moral of the Story:

Believing in God's plans can bring unexpected joys. Patience and faith are powerful and can lead to wonderful blessings.

Chapter 35

Moses and Aaron's River Rescue

Once upon a time, in a vast, sunlit valley surrounded by towering mountains, there lived two brothers, Moses and Aaron. They were not just any brothers; they were kind, brave, and loved by all who knew them. Moses was wise and thoughtful, while Aaron was cheerful and spoke well. Together, they made a great team.

In this valley, there was a big problem—the river that flowed through it, giving water to all the plants, animals, and people, had suddenly stopped flowing. The ground began to dry up, flowers wilted, and the trees lost their green leaves. The animals grew thirsty, and the people were worried. Everyone in the valley was trying to find out why the river had stopped and how to bring the water back.

One day, Moses and Aaron decided that they would go on an adventure to find the source of the river and fix whatever was wrong. They packed some food, took their staffs, and started walking towards the mountains from where the river used to flow.

As they journeyed, they climbed steep paths, crossed small streams, and walked through large fields of flowers. After many days of travel, they finally reached a high place where they could see a large lake. But to their surprise, a huge pile of rocks blocked the water from flowing down into the valley.

Moses and Aaron knew they had to remove the rocks to save their valley. They started by trying to move the rocks with their hands, but they were too heavy. They tried using sticks to pry the rocks away, but the sticks broke. It seemed impossible, but they didn't give up.

That night, as they sat near the lake under the stars, Moses had an idea. "Let's ask for help," he said. "Tomorrow, let's invite all the animals of the mountains to help us." Aaron thought it was a great idea.

The next morning, Moses and Aaron called out to the mountain animals. Soon, their call was answered. Eagles, bears, goats, and even small creatures like rabbits and squirrels came. Moses and Aaron explained their problem, and all the animals agreed to help.

Together, they all worked as a team. The bears used their strength to move the heavier rocks, the eagles and the squirrels slipped through small gaps to push smaller stones, and the goats kicked away the pebbles. Aaron cheered everyone on, and Moses made sure everyone was safe and working together.

By sunset, the pile of rocks was cleared, and the water began to flow again. It rushed down the mountainside, back into the valley. The river was alive once more! The plants perked up, the animals drank happily, and the people of the valley cheered with joy.

Moses and Aaron thanked all the animals for their help. They had all worked together to solve a big problem, and in doing so, they had made many new friends.

The news of the flowing river spread quickly, and soon the valley was filled with laughter and celebration. The people planted new flowers, and the trees started to grow green leaves again. The valley, once dry and sad, was now vibrant and full of life.

As the sun set on their happy valley, Moses and Aaron looked at each other with pride. They knew that they had done something wonderful. They had brought their community together and shown everyone the power of unity and teamwork.

Moral of the Story:

Working together can solve big problems. Teamwork and kindness bring communities together and make them stronger.

Chapter 36

Prophet Idris and the Angel Gabriel

In a land of gentle hills and blooming meadows, there lived a wise and patient man named Idris. Unlike anyone else in his village, Idris was a chosen prophet of God. He was revered not just for his deep wisdom but also for his unwavering devotion to spreading messages of love and faith.

Every day, Idris would walk through the lush fields, surrounded by the beauty of nature. He loved to reflect on the wonders of God's creation. Often, he found peace sitting by the riverside, watching the water flow and listening to the leaves rustling in the breeze.

One serene day, while Idris was deep in prayer beside the river, a remarkable event happened. The angel Gabriel appeared before him, bringing a message from God. Gabriel told Idris that he had been chosen as a prophet. His mission was to guide people and share God's teachings of love and peace.

Overwhelmed with humility and gratitude, Idris accepted this divine task. With a heart full of love, he set out to fulfill God's command. Idris began to travel across the lands, meeting people from different villages. Wherever he went, he spread messages of peace, kindness, and compassion.

Idris taught everyone about the importance of having faith, being patient, and living humbly. He showed them how to pray sincerely, how to treat others with respect and kindness, and how to be thankful for the many blessings they had. Idris's words were simple but powerful, and they touched the hearts of those who listened.

Despite his wisdom, Idris's journey was not without challenges. He faced many obstacles and trials, but he never lost faith. Whenever he felt overwhelmed, he prayed for strength and guidance. Idris trusted in God's plan, knowing that he was being guided every step of the way.

One day, Idris came across a village where the people were struggling with a terrible drought. The fields were dry, the rivers had stopped flowing, and the people and animals were very thirsty. Seeing their plight, Idris felt deep compassion and knelt down to pray. He asked God to bless the land with rain.

Miraculously, dark clouds began to gather in the sky, and soon, it started to rain. The villagers rejoiced as the rainwater filled their rivers and watered their fields. They were grateful to Idris for his prayers and thanked him for bringing hope and relief.

As he continued his mission, Idris's influence grew. He inspired many people to follow the path of goodness and faith. He demonstrated that even during times of hardship and uncertainty, the love and mercy of God were always present for those who believed and trusted in His wisdom.

Idris also taught the importance of knowledge and learning. He encouraged the people to seek knowledge and to use it to better their lives and the lives of others. He showed them how to read and write, and how to use their skills to build a stronger, more united community.

Years passed, and Idris's teachings spread far and wide. His life's work had a profound impact on many, guiding them towards a life of righteousness and peace. People remembered him not only as a prophet but as a kind teacher who taught them how to live better lives.

Moral of the Story:

Wisdom and patience are key to overcoming life's challenges. By trusting in God's plan and spreading kindness, we can make a positive difference in the world.

Chapter 37

Isaiah and the Special Message

ISAIAH AND THE SPECIAL MESSAGE

Once upon a time, in a land of rolling hills and deep valleys, there lived a kind man named Isaiah. Isaiah was no ordinary man; he had a very special job as a prophet. This meant he received messages from God to share with the people around him.

One bright, sunny morning, Isaiah was strolling through a beautiful garden filled with colorful flowers and singing birds when he heard a gentle voice. It was God speaking to him! God told Isaiah that he needed to help the people in his town become better and kinder to each other.

In Isaiah's town, people often forgot to be nice. They didn't share their toys, sometimes they ignored those in need, and occasionally, they said unkind words. God wanted Isaiah to remind everyone of the importance of caring for each other and living in peace.

Isaiah listened carefully to God's message. A warm glow filled his heart, knowing he had a very important mission. Eager to fulfill this task, he returned to his town and began speaking to everyone he met.

Isaiah shared stories about kindness, sharing, and love. He explained how important it was to treat friends and even strangers with respect and compassion. His words were soothing and wise, and people started to listen.

Gradually, the town began to change. Children started sharing their toys more and helped each other during playtime. Adults became more helpful to their neighbors and shared their resources with those less fortunate. The town was becoming a warmer, more welcoming place.

Isaiah was overjoyed to see these positive changes. He continued to spread messages of kindness and love everywhere he went. However, his job wasn't always easy. Sometimes people didn't listen, or they quickly forgot his words. But Isaiah never gave up. He believed that with patience and faith, everything could improve.

One day, Isaiah decided to do something special to bring the whole town together. He suggested having a big feast where everyone could share their food and celebrate their community. The townspeople loved the idea and started preparing for the grand event.

On the day of the feast, the town square was decorated with colorful ribbons and flowers. Long tables were set up, filled with delicious food. There were apples from the orchards, freshly baked bread, and bouquets of flowers from the gardens. The townspeople brought their best dishes and gathered with smiles and laughter.

Isaiah watched with a smile, feeling grateful and happy because he knew his hard work had helped bring everyone together. As the people ate and enjoyed each other's company, they remembered Isaiah's words about kindness and sharing. They saw how wonderful it felt to be united and caring.

From that day forward, the town was filled with more laughter and kindness than ever before. The people helped each other more, and there was a strong sense of community. They continued to follow Isaiah's teachings, making sure to pass them down to their children.

As the years passed, Isaiah continued to share his messages with new generations. Even as he grew very old, his heart stayed warm and joyful because he knew he had made a significant difference in his community. His teachings lived on, and the town remained a place of peace and harmony.

Moral of the Story:

Kindness and faith have the power to change hearts and bring people together, creating a community filled with harmony and peace.

Chapter 38
King Solomon's Flying Carpet

In a magical kingdom filled with wonders, there lived a wise and just king named Solomon. Unlike any ordinary king, Solomon was blessed with unique gifts from God. He could communicate with animals and birds and even control the winds!

One day, King Solomon received an extraordinary gift—a huge, magnificent flying carpet. This was no ordinary carpet. It was bright red with golden threads woven through it, and it had the magical ability to fly through the sky as swiftly as the wind. The carpet was so large it could carry not only Solomon but his entire army, his courtiers, and all his royal animals!

King Solomon saw the flying carpet as a way to explore the world. He wanted to visit distant lands to spread messages of peace and understanding and to learn about cultures different from his own.

One sunny morning, Solomon gathered his people for their first adventure on the flying carpet. With just a command, the carpet softly lifted off the ground, soaring high above mountains, rivers, and bustling cities. People below gazed up in amazement, marveling at the sight of a flying carpet above them.

Their first destination was a land suffering from a terrible drought. The fields were barren, and the people were hungry and desolate. Seeing their plight, King Solomon felt deep compassion. He spoke to the wind, requesting it to bring rain to the parched land. Soon, clouds gathered overhead, and rain began to nourish the earth below. The local people danced and celebrated, thanking Solomon for his miraculous help.

As their journey continued, Solomon and his companions encountered various tribes and nations. In each place, Solomon shared his wisdom about fairness and kindness. He listened to the people's troubles and helped them find solutions, whether it was resolving a dispute between neighbors or advising on how to protect forests and rivers.

One day, they reached a land where the people were very sad because their beautiful garden had been ruined by a fierce storm. The trees were uprooted, and the flowers were destroyed. Solomon's magical animals pitched in to help. His birds gathered seeds and planted them, while his lions and elephants helped replant the trees. The garden began to flourish once again, bringing joy back to the people.

Solomon also taught the children of each village he visited. He would sit with them, sharing stories and lessons about the importance of being kind, honest, and helpful. The children loved listening to him and promised to follow his teachings.

After many months of traveling and helping others, Solomon and his entourage returned to their kingdom. They brought back stories and gifts from all the lands they had visited, which excited the people of Solomon's kingdom.

King Solomon shared lessons from his travels, teaching his people about the importance of understanding different cultures and assisting those in need. He showed them that by working together, everyone could contribute to making the world a better place.

The flying carpet became a cherished symbol of unity and adventure in Solomon's kingdom. It reminded everyone that despite distances or differences in lifestyle, they were all connected by threads of humanity and kindness.

Moral of the Story:

Cooperation and understanding among different cultures can create a world full of respect and shared prosperity. By helping others, we can make the world a better place for everyone.

Chapter 39

Muhammad and the Spider

Long ago, in a desert land filled with sand dunes and sprawling oases, there lived a kind and wise man named Muhammad. He was known throughout his homeland for his gentleness and fairness. Many people loved him and followed his teachings about kindness and love. However, not everyone agreed with his ideas, and some did not want things to change.

One day, Muhammad and his close friend Abu Bakr found themselves in great danger. Some people in their town were very upset with them and wanted to harm them because of their beliefs. To stay safe, Muhammad and Abu Bakr knew they needed to find a hiding place and come up with a plan.

They chose to take refuge in a small cave on a nearby mountain. This cave was a quiet, hidden spot where they hoped to be safe for a while. As they entered the cave, they were both worried but trusted that God would protect them.

Outside, the angry crowd was searching high and low. They came closer and closer to the mountain where Muhammad and Abu Bakr were hiding. The two friends were very anxious but kept their faith strong, praying for safety.

Just then, something remarkable happened. A little spider began to spin a web at the entrance of the cave. It spun quickly and skillfully, weaving its web back and forth until the entire entrance was covered. The web looked delicate but was strong enough to cover the whole opening. At the same time, a dove flew down and laid its eggs right at the cave's entrance, settling in as if it had been there for a long time.

When the searching crowd reached the cave, they saw the spider's web and the dove with its eggs. They thought to themselves, "Surely, no one could have entered this cave recently without breaking this delicate web or disturbing these eggs." Convinced that the cave was empty, they decided not to search inside and moved on.

Inside the cave, Muhammad and Abu Bakr felt a deep sense of relief and gratitude. They realized that the spider's web and the dove's nest were signs of divine protection. They stayed hidden in the cave for three days, spending their time in prayer and planning their next steps. When it finally felt safe, they left the cave and continued their journey. They traveled until they reached a place where they were welcomed and could live in peace.

Muhammad often shared the story of the spider and the dove with others, teaching them valuable lessons. He reminded them that no act of kindness is too small and that help can come from the most unexpected places.

As the years passed, the story of Muhammad and the protective spider became a beloved tale told to children and adults alike. It inspired many to be brave and to trust that even in the most challenging times, there is always hope and help.

In the peaceful town where Muhammad and Abu Bakr finally settled, the people lived happily, knowing they were part of a story filled with faith and miracles. They built a beautiful mosque where everyone could come together to pray and share stories of courage and kindness.

Moral of the Story:

Even the smallest acts of kindness can make a big difference. Faith and courage can bring miraculous help in difficult times.

Chapter 40

King Solomon and the Playful Jinn

Once upon a time, in a land of sprawling sand dunes and lush oases, there lived a wise and kind king named Solomon. King Solomon was no ordinary king; he possessed extraordinary gifts. He could understand and speak with animals, command the wind, and even converse with jinns, mysterious beings from an unseen world.

King Solomon was a fair and just ruler who cared deeply for all creatures, big and small. He always listened to their problems with great patience and wisdom. One bright and sunny morning, as he strolled through his beautiful gardens, King Solomon noticed an unusual commotion. The birds chirped louder than usual, and the trees seemed to whisper among themselves, signaling distress.

Intrigued, King Solomon called upon the wind to explain the disturbance. The wind, responding with a gentle breeze, told him that a mischievous jinn was at the heart of the trouble. This playful jinn enjoyed tricking the animals and disturbing the plants, causing quite a stir in the peaceful garden.

Determined to resolve the issue, King Solomon decided to summon the jinn. With a puff of smoke and a playful swirl, the jinn appeared before him. The jinn was a lively creature, with twinkling eyes and a cheeky grin, exuding an air of mischief.

King Solomon addressed him kindly, "Why do you disturb the peace of my garden?"

The jinn giggled and replied, "Oh mighty King, I mean no harm. I simply find joy in playing tricks! It's so much fun!"

The king pondered for a moment and then spoke, "Playing is indeed wonderful, but it is also important to respect others. How would you feel if someone played a trick on you that you didn't enjoy?"

The jinn paused, scratching his head, a new thought dawning on him. "I suppose I wouldn't like it very much," he admitted.

King Solomon smiled warmly, an idea forming in his wise mind. "What if you use your cleverness to help rather than hinder? You can still play and have fun, but in a way that brings joy to others instead of trouble."

Intrigued by this new way of thinking, the jinn agreed to try. King Solomon then tasked him with activities that utilized his unique abilities and love for mischief, but in helpful and joyful ways. The jinn began to find lost treasures, play amusing games with the royal children, and entertain guests with his antics—all the while ensuring everyone was laughing and enjoying themselves.

The jinn helped the gardeners by using his magic to water the plants during dry spells and to make the flowers bloom even more brilliantly. He became friends with the animals, playing gentle games with them and making sure they were always happy and safe.

As time passed, the mischievous jinn transformed into one of King Solomon's most trusted helpers. He discovered that making others happy brought him more joy than any of his previous tricks ever did.

Peace and happiness returned to the garden. The animals thrived, the plants grew lush and green, and everyone in King Solomon's kingdom benefited from the harmony and understanding that now reigned.

Moral of the Story:

Understanding others and finding positive ways to use our abilities can bring joy and harmony to everyone around us.

Chapter 41

Moses and the Twelve Springs

MOSES AND THE TWELVE SPRINGS

Long ago, in a vast sun-drenched desert, there lived a wise and kind man named Moses. He was not just any man; Moses was a leader, chosen to guide his people through endless sands and rocky terrains on a long journey to find a new home where they could live happily and safely.

As they traveled under the scorching sun, the desert seemed to stretch infinitely, with nothing but sand in every direction. The days grew increasingly hot, and their water supplies dwindled. Thirsty and tired, the people began to worry. They gathered around Moses, their faces lined with weariness and concern.

"Moses, we are thirsty," they lamented. "Please help us find water."

Feeling a deep responsibility and care for his people, Moses wanted to alleviate their suffering. With a heart full of compassion, he prayed fervently, seeking assistance to quench the thirst of his followers.

As Moses concluded his prayer, a remarkable event unfolded. Guided by his unwavering faith, he struck a large rock with his staff as instructed by divine inspiration. To everyone's astonishment, a miracle occurred—twelve beautiful springs of cool, clear water burst forth from the rock!

The people were astounded and overjoyed. They rushed to the springs, filling their cups and bottles, and splashing the refreshing water on their faces. Laughter and cheerful chatter soon filled the air as each of the twelve tribes chose a spring to drink from.

With their thirst quenched, the atmosphere among the people transformed. Worry turned into joy, and exhaustion into energy. They danced and sang around the springs, expressing their gratitude for this miraculous blessing.

Moses watched over his people with a gentle smile, relieved and pleased to see them so happy. He knew that their journey had taught them valuable lessons about the power of faith and the importance of unity when facing great challenges.

The twelve springs continued to flow, each a symbol of the strength they found in staying together and supporting one another. With their spirits renewed, the people were ready to resume their trek across the desert, confident that together, they could overcome any obstacle.

As the years passed, the story of Moses and the twelve springs was passed down from generation to generation. It served as a lasting reminder of the power of hope, faith, and unity.

Moral of the Story:

Unity and faith can lead to miraculous solutions. Together, we are stronger and can overcome great challenges.

Chapter 42

The Wise Words of Muhammad

A long time ago, in a faraway place called Mecca, there lived a man named Muhammad. Muhammad was very special. He was always kind, honest, and wise. Everyone in the city trusted him and called him "Al-Amin," which means "the trustworthy." People knew they could count on Muhammad to tell the truth and help others.

Muhammad liked to spend time thinking about the world and the stars in the sky. He often went to a small cave on a mountain near Mecca. In the quiet cave, he could be alone to think and meditate. He felt peaceful and calm there.

One night, something amazing happened while Muhammad was in the cave. It was a night that would change his life forever. As he sat in the quiet cave, he suddenly felt a presence. He looked up and saw an angel! The angel filled the cave with a warm and gentle light. Muhammad was surprised and a little scared, but the angel's calmness made him feel better.

The angel spoke in a clear and beautiful voice, "Read!" But Muhammad was confused because he had never learned to read.

"I cannot read," Muhammad replied humbly.

The angel gently embraced him and repeated, "Read in the name of your Lord who created all things."

With these words, a deep understanding filled Muhammad's heart. Suddenly, he could recite beautiful and wise words. These words were not his own but were given to him in that magical moment. They taught about kindness, truth, and the importance of caring for each other.

This was the first of many messages that Muhammad would receive over his lifetime. These messages came to be known as the Quran. They taught people how to live together in peace and respect each other.

After this first revelation, Muhammad felt a great responsibility. He knew he must share these important words with others. He returned to Mecca and began teaching what he had learned. Not everyone wanted to listen at first, but Muhammad's kindness and honesty won their hearts over time.

People began to gather around Muhammad to hear the wise words. They learned that everyone should be treated with respect, that kindness is stronger than anger, and that taking care of the poor and needy is very important.

As more people listened to Muhammad, they started to understand his teachings. They saw how his words could help them live better lives. More and more people came to learn about the messages of peace and respect that were taught in the Quran. These teachings helped people from different places and backgrounds live together in harmony.

Muhammad continued to share his messages for many years. He traveled to different places, always speaking with kindness and wisdom. People loved and respected him because he was always fair and just.

Through his words and actions, Muhammad showed everyone the importance of being good and kind. His teachings spread far and wide, bringing peace and harmony to many people.

Moral of the Story:

Great wisdom often comes when we seek quiet moments for reflection. By sharing important messages, we can bring light and understanding into the world.

Chapter 43

The Journey to Mecca

A long time ago, in a sunny desert land, there lived a kind and wise man named Muhammad. He was not just any man; he was a Prophet, which means he was special because he shared messages from Allah with people to help them live better lives.

Prophet Muhammad lived in a beautiful city called Medina with his friends and followers. They were all very close, like a big, happy family. One day, Prophet Muhammad decided it was time to visit a very special place called Kaaba in the city of Mecca. It was a peaceful journey they wanted to make, to pray and be close to Allah.

However, reaching Mecca was not easy. There was a group of people from Mecca called the Quraysh who were not very friendly at that time. They didn't want Prophet Muhammad and his followers to enter the city. When Muhammad and his followers got close, the Quraysh stopped them. They were not allowed to go any further.

But Prophet Muhammad was very wise. He knew that fighting was not the answer. Instead, he wanted to talk and find a peaceful way. So, he sent his friend, Uthman, to discuss with the leaders of Mecca and find a solution. While waiting for Uthman to return, everyone was very anxious and hoped for good news.

After some time, Uthman came back with a message. The Quraysh had agreed to make a deal called the Pact of Hudaibiyah. This deal was a promise between the two groups. The main points of the deal were:

1. Prophet Muhammad and his followers would go back to Medina without visiting Kaaba that year.

2. They could come back next year and stay in Mecca for three days to pray.

3. There would be no fighting between the two groups for ten whole years.

Some of Prophet Muhammad's followers were sad and disappointed. They had traveled a long way and wanted to visit Kaaba so badly. But Prophet Muhammad reassured them that this agreement was a good thing. He explained that avoiding fighting and making friends was much better and would help everyone live peacefully.

Prophet Muhammad's trust in Allah and his choice to make a peaceful pact showed everyone how important it is to be patient and to solve problems without fighting. They all learned that sometimes, not getting what you want immediately can lead to better things in the future.

And just as promised, the next year, Prophet Muhammad and his followers returned to Mecca peacefully. They prayed at Kaaba and were happy. The people of Mecca saw that the followers of Prophet Muhammad were kind and trustworthy, which made them respect him even more.

Sometimes, when things don't go as planned, being patient and finding peaceful solutions can lead to better outcomes. It teaches us the power of making promises and keeping them, and how kindness and patience can bring people together.

Moral of the Story:

Being patient and finding peaceful solutions can lead to better outcomes. Kindness and patience can bring people together.

Chapter 44

Moses and the Golden Calf

Long, long ago, there was a wise man named Moses. He was a leader chosen to guide his people to a better life. Moses was very kind and always tried to teach his people good things.

One day, Moses told his people that he needed to go up a high mountain to speak with God. He wanted to receive special rules that would help everyone live better together. So, he left his brother Aaron in charge and began his climb up the mountain.

Moses was gone for many days. While he was away, the people started to feel worried and scared. They wondered, "Where has Moses gone? Why is he taking so long?" They felt so confused without Moses there to guide them.

Seeing this, some of the people came up with a not-so-good idea. They decided to make a statue of a calf out of gold and said, "This golden calf is our guide now!" They thought if they had something they could see and touch, they wouldn't feel so scared.

Aaron saw what was happening and felt very stuck. He didn't want to make the golden calf, but he also didn't want the people to feel scared. So, he hoped that by letting them make the calf, they would feel better until Moses came back.

However, making the golden calf didn't really solve their problem. It just made things more confusing! When Moses came back down from the mountain, he was very surprised and sad to see his people dancing around the golden calf. He had been so excited to share the special rules he received from God, which were meant to help everyone live happily and peacefully.

Seeing the golden calf, Moses showed the people how their choice hadn't helped them but had made things worse. The people quickly realized their mistake. They felt very sorry because they understood that instead of waiting patiently for Moses, they had chosen a quick fix that didn't work at all.

Moses forgave them and reminded them that it's important to trust and be patient, even when things seem unsure or take a long time. With this lesson learned, they all promised to try their best to wait and trust in what's right, even when it's hard.

Moses then shared the special rules he had received from God. These rules were written on stone tablets and were called the Ten Commandments. The people listened carefully as Moses explained each rule. They learned that these rules would help them live together in peace and harmony.

The first rule was to always remember and respect God.

The second rule was to never make or worship idols, like the golden calf.

The third rule was to always speak truthfully and respectfully about God.

The fourth rule was to keep one day each week special for rest and prayer.

The fifth rule was to respect their parents.

The sixth rule was to never hurt others.

The seventh rule was to always be faithful and loving to their families.

The eighth rule was to never take things that didn't belong to them.

The ninth rule was to always tell the truth.

The tenth rule was to be happy with what they had and not be jealous of others.

The people listened and understood how important these rules were. They promised to follow them and live by them. They realized that by following these rules, they could live in a way that made everyone feel safe, respected, and happy.

Moses was glad to see that his people had learned a valuable lesson. They had learned that patience and trust were very important. They understood that rushing to find quick solutions, like making the golden calf, was not the right way.

With these new rules and a promise to be patient and trust in what is right, Moses and his people continued their journey. They felt stronger and more united than ever before.

Moral of the Story:

Being patient and trusting in what is right helps us make better choices. Quick fixes can lead to mistakes, but patience brings true guidance.

Chapter 45

Moses and the Sweet Spring

MOSES AND THE SWEET SPRING

Once upon a time, in a sun-drenched desert, there traveled a group of people led by a kind and wise man named Moses. Moses had been chosen to guide these people, known as the Israelites, to a safe new home across vast and challenging lands.

One hot and dusty day, after walking under the blazing sun, the people grew very thirsty. Their water bottles were empty, and the children's voices grew tired from asking, "When will we drink?" Everyone's hopes were drooping like the leaves on a thirsty plant.

Finally, they came upon a spring. Oh, how their hearts leaped with joy! But when the first person dipped his cup into the water and took a drink, he spat it out. "This water is bitter!" he exclaimed. One by one, others tried the water, only to find it too bitter to drink. The disappointment was as heavy as the hot air around them.

Seeing his people so unhappy and knowing how much they needed water, Moses turned to God for help. He asked, "Please help us, for the water is bitter and my people are very thirsty."

God listened to Moses' sincere request and showed him a special piece of wood nearby. God instructed Moses to throw this wood into the bitter water. Moses, trusting God's wisdom, did just as he was told.

To everyone's amazement, as soon as the wood touched the water, it began to clear and sweeten. What was once bitter now became deliciously sweet! The people rushed to drink, filling their cups with water that refreshed them body and soul. The children laughed and splashed, their spirits lifted by the miraculous change.

The people drank until they were satisfied. They filled their bottles and shared the water with their animals. Everyone was happy and refreshed. They knew that this was a special blessing given to them because of Moses' faith and God's love.

As they continued their journey, the memory of the sweet spring stayed with them. Whenever they faced hard times, they remembered how the bitter water had turned sweet. This gave them hope and strength to keep going, knowing that even when things seemed difficult, there was always a way to find relief.

Moses continued to lead his people through many challenges. There were times when they felt scared or unsure, but Moses always reminded them of the sweet spring. He told them that just as the water had been changed, their problems could also be solved with patience and faith.

One day, after a long and tiring walk, they reached a beautiful oasis. There were palm trees, shady spots to rest, and plenty of sweet water to drink. The people were overjoyed. They set up their tents and rested, feeling grateful and happy.

Moses gathered everyone together and spoke to them. He reminded them of the bitter spring that had turned sweet. He told them that their journey would have many more challenges, but they should always remember that help and guidance were always near.

The people listened and promised to keep faith and trust in their hearts. They knew that as long as they followed Moses and believed in God's help, they would reach their new home safely.

Moral of the Story:

Even when things seem difficult, having faith and following wise guidance can turn challenges into blessings. Patience and trust can transform hardship into relief.

Chapter 46

Muhammad and the Unity Pact

In a bustling city called Medina, there lived a kind and wise man named Muhammad. He was chosen to guide the people and show them how to live together peacefully, no matter their differences.

Medina was a place where people of different backgrounds, beliefs, and tribes lived. Some were Muslims who followed Muhammad, while others believed in different things. The city was like a patchwork quilt, made up of many colorful pieces.

Muhammad knew that for the city to thrive, everyone needed to work together and respect each other's ways. So, he gathered all the people in a big meeting. He sat down with them and talked about how they could live in harmony and help each other.

At this meeting, Muhammad put forward something very special called the Charter of Medina. This charter was like a promise—a promise that all the people of Medina would support each other, no matter where they came from or what they believed.

In this charter, Muhammad made sure that everyone had the right to practice their own faith and traditions. He also made sure that if anyone tried to harm the city or its people, everyone would come together to protect it.

The people agreed to this charter with joy in their hearts. They understood that by working together and respecting each other, they could build a strong and peaceful community. From that day on, Medina became a shining example of diversity and unity.

The people of Medina lived side by side, helping each other in times of need and celebrating together in times of joy. Muhammad's teachings of peace, kindness, and understanding became the guiding light for everyone in Medina.

One sunny morning, a traveler from a faraway land arrived in Medina. He was amazed to see how the people lived together so happily. He saw Muslims, Christians, and Jews all talking and working together. He saw children from different backgrounds playing together, sharing their toys and games.

The traveler went to Muhammad and asked, "How did you make this city so peaceful and united?"

Muhammad smiled and said, "We made a promise to each other. We promised to respect and support one another, no matter our differences. We agreed to work together and protect each other. This promise is called the Charter of Medina."

The traveler was very impressed. He asked if he could stay in Medina and learn more about how to live in such a wonderful way. Muhammad welcomed him with open arms and invited him to be a part of their community.

Days turned into weeks, and the traveler saw how the people of Medina lived out the principles of the Charter every day. He saw neighbors helping each other, sharing their food, and celebrating together. He saw how everyone had a role to play in keeping the city safe and happy.

The traveler was so inspired that he decided to take the message of unity and peace back to his own land. He wanted to share what he had learned with others so that they too could live in harmony.

Moral of the Story:

Working together and respecting each other, no matter our differences, helps us build strong and peaceful communities. Unity and kindness make us stronger and bring us happiness.

Chapter 47

Abraham's Journey of Faith

In the land of ancient times, there lived a man named Abraham. Abraham was known for his strong faith in God. He loved to think about the wonders of the world and wanted to understand more about life and death. Every evening, Abraham would gaze up at the sky filled with twinkling stars, feeling a deep longing in his heart to learn more about God's creation.

One night, as Abraham looked at the stars, he prayed to God. He asked God for a sign to strengthen his faith and bring him peace. Abraham wanted to know how God created and sustained all living things, from the tiniest ant to the majestic birds flying high above.

God heard Abraham's sincere prayer and decided to show him a miraculous lesson through the birds. One day, God spoke to Abraham and asked him to gather four different types of birds: a crow, a rooster, a dove, and a peacock. Abraham followed God's instructions and brought the birds to him with great care and respect.

God then told Abraham to place each bird on a separate hill. Abraham did as he was told and watched as the birds perched on their hills. Then, God asked Abraham to call the birds back to him.

Abraham called out to the birds with a loud voice. To his surprise, only the dove responded and returned to him. The crow, the rooster, and the peacock stayed on their hills. God then told Abraham to watch what happened next.

As Abraham looked on, he saw something amazing. The crow, the rooster, and the peacock suddenly fell down lifeless. It was as if God was showing Abraham the cycle of life and death, teaching him about the fragility and beauty of existence. Abraham was amazed and a little sad, but he kept watching closely.

Then, God performed a great miracle. Before Abraham's eyes, the crow, the rooster, and the peacock came back to life and flew back to him. The birds were alive again, showing that God has the power over life and death. Abraham was filled with awe and wonder at this miraculous sight.

The dove, which had returned to Abraham first, symbolized the enduring spirit of life that God gives to all living creatures. Through this powerful demonstration, Abraham gained a deeper understanding of God's infinite wisdom and mercy. He realized that life and death are both part of God's plan and that every living being has its time under God's care.

Abraham felt a sense of peace and reassurance in his faith. He understood that just as the birds had their time on earth, so did all living beings. He knew that God was always with him, guiding him and taking care of everything.

With a heart full of gratitude, Abraham continued his journey. His faith was stronger than ever, and he trusted in God's plan completely. He appreciated the marvels of creation around him and felt a deep connection to all living things.

Moral of the Story:

Through faith and reflection, we can find comfort and understanding in the mysteries of life and death. God's wisdom guides us through every moment of our existence.

Chapter 48

Moses and the Missing Robe

In a bustling town, there lived a man named Moses, known for his wisdom and kindness. One bright morning, as Moses was walking through the market, he noticed a commotion near the marketplace. Curious, he approached to see what was happening.

A young man was standing in the center, looking worried. He explained to Moses that someone had stolen his precious robe while he was shopping for goods in the market. The young man was upset because the robe was a gift from his father, and he cherished it dearly.

Moses listened carefully to the young man's story and saw the sadness in his eyes. He then turned to the crowd and asked if anyone had seen what happened or knew anything about the missing robe. The people shook their heads, unsure of who could have taken it.

Feeling a sense of responsibility to help, Moses decided to investigate further. He asked the merchants and shoppers if they had noticed anything unusual that day. After talking to several people, one elderly lady approached Moses hesitantly.

The lady whispered to Moses that she had seen a young boy leaving the market with a robe that looked similar to the one described by the young man. She pointed in the direction where the boy had gone.

With determination, Moses followed the lady's lead and eventually found the young boy wearing the stolen robe. The boy was scared and ashamed when Moses approached him. Moses asked gently, "Why did you take this robe? It belongs to someone else."

The boy hesitated but then tearfully confessed that he had taken the robe without permission because he did not have warm clothes for the upcoming winter. He felt sorry for what he had done and regretted his actions.

Moses understood the boy's problem and saw that he had acted out of need rather than malice. He then turned to the young man and explained what had happened. The young man, moved by the boy's honesty, forgave him and even offered him help for his clothing needs.

Through this incident, Moses taught everyone present about the importance of honesty, compassion, and forgiveness. He showed that even in difficult situations, it is essential to speak the truth, seek understanding, and show kindness to one another.

The town learned from Moses' example that justice is not just about punishing wrongdoings but also about understanding circumstances, showing mercy, and helping those in need.

Moses was happy to see the change in the community. People began to look out for one another and help each other in times of need. The market became a place filled with laughter and joy, where everyone felt safe and cared for.

From that day on, the town became known for its kindness and generosity. People came from far and wide to see the wonderful community where everyone helped each other. Moses continued to guide the people with his wisdom and kindness, ensuring that the spirit of honesty, compassion, and forgiveness lived on.

Moral of the Story:

Honesty, compassion, and forgiveness are important values that help us understand and support one another. By being kind and understanding, we can create a caring and just community.

Chapter 49

Luqman's Lessons of Wisdom

LUQMAN'S LESSONS OF WISDOM

In a peaceful village, there lived a man named Luqman, known far and wide for his wisdom and kind heart. Luqman was a humble man who carried great knowledge within his gentle soul. He loved helping people and sharing what he knew.

One sunny day, Luqman's young son came to him with curious eyes. He wanted to learn the secrets of his father's wisdom. Seeing how eager his son was to learn, Luqman decided to share his most important lessons. They sat down together under the shade of a grand tree, ready for a special talk.

"Listen carefully, my dear son," Luqman began. "The most precious gift we have is the ability to talk to God through prayer. Always remember to pray and say thank you for the blessings in your life. Prayer is like a gentle breeze that makes our hearts feel happy and close to God."

Luqman's son nodded, eager to learn more. Luqman continued, "Patience is another important virtue. In times of difficulty and challenges, remember to be patient and trust in God's plan. Just like a tiny seed waits for the rain to grow into a mighty tree, patience helps us grow strong and wise."

As they talked, a little bird landed on a branch above them, singing a sweet melody. Luqman pointed to the bird and said, "See how the bird sings with joy? Humility is like that bird's song—it brings lightness to the heart and peace to the soul. Stay humble, my son, for humility helps us learn and understand more."

Luqman's son listened carefully and felt grateful for the valuable lessons he was receiving. He realized that wisdom was not just about knowing things but also about living with a pure heart and a clear conscience.

Days turned into weeks, and Luqman's son began to practice his father's teachings in his daily life. He prayed every day, found strength in patience, and tried to stay humble. He noticed that his heart felt lighter, his mind sharper, and his spirit more peaceful.

One day, a group of children in the village were arguing over a game. Luqman's son remembered his father's lessons and went over to help. "Let's play together and take turns," he suggested with a kind smile. The children agreed, and soon everyone was laughing and playing happily.

Another time, Luqman's son saw an old woman struggling to carry her heavy basket. Remembering his father's words about helping others, he quickly ran over to assist her. The old woman thanked him with a warm smile, and Luqman's son felt a deep sense of joy from his act of kindness.

People from near and far started coming to Luqman's home seeking advice and guidance. They marveled at the wisdom that flowed from Luqman and touched their hearts with its simplicity and depth. Luqman always welcomed them with open arms and shared his knowledge generously.

Moral of the Story:

Through prayer, patience, and humility, we unlock the doors to wisdom and understanding that illuminate our path and enrich the lives of those around us.

Chapter 50

Moses and the Scared Servant

In a land of ancient wonders, there lived a great man named Moses. He was chosen by God to guide his people through many challenges and hardships.

One day, as Moses was traveling through the desert with his companions, they came across a frightened servant who was trembling with fear. The servant had lost his way and was alone in the vast wilderness, unsure of where to go.

Seeing the fear in the servant's eyes, Moses approached him with a gentle smile and asked, "Why are you so scared, my friend? How can I help you?" The servant explained that he had become separated from his group and was afraid of being lost in the desert.

Moses listened attentively to the servant's story and felt compassion for him. He reassured the servant that he would not abandon him and that together, they would find a way back to safety.

With Moses leading the way, they journeyed through the desert, with the sun shining brightly above them.

As they walked, they faced many challenges—a steep hill to climb, a narrow path to cross, and a rocky terrain to navigate. Despite the obstacles, Moses remained steadfast and guided the servant with patience and care.

While climbing the steep hill, the servant stumbled and fell. Moses quickly helped him up and said, "Don't worry, we will make it together." The servant felt grateful for Moses' support and continued to follow him with renewed determination.

When they reached the narrow path, the servant hesitated, feeling scared of the heights. Moses held his hand and gently guided him across. "You are not alone," Moses said, "We can do this together." The servant felt his fear fade away as he trusted Moses' guidance.

Next, they came upon the rocky terrain. The servant was tired and his feet hurt, but Moses encouraged him, saying, "We are almost there. Keep going, and we will find a safe place to rest." The servant took a deep breath and pushed forward, inspired by Moses' unwavering support.

Finally, after their long and challenging journey, they reached their destination. The servant looked at Moses with gratitude in his eyes. He thanked Moses for his kindness, courage, and leadership that had brought them safely through the desert.

Moses smiled at the servant and replied, "Do not fear, my friend, for God is always with us, guiding us through our darkest moments. Together, we can overcome any obstacle and find our way to safety."

The servant felt a sense of peace wash over him as he realized the truth in Moses' words. He learned that with faith, courage, and the support of others, even the most daunting challenges could be overcome.

From that day on, the servant carried with him the memory of Moses' compassion and bravery. He became a source of inspiration for others, sharing the story of how a kind-hearted leader had guided him through his fears and led him to safety.

Moral of the Story:

Through compassion, courage, and guidance,
we can navigate through fear and uncertainty.
With faith and support, we can overcome any
obstacle on our path.

www.ingramcontent.com/pod-product-compliance
Lightning Source LLC
Chambersburg PA
CBHW051210290426
44109CB00021B/2404